NIGHTFALL

Soul Harvest

TODD TOMASELLA

Copyright © 2016
Todd Tomasella
All rights reserved.

SafeGuardYourSoul.com
Frisco, Texas
Visit SafeGuardYourSoul.com

© *Todd Tomasella. All Rights Reserved.*

Any part of this book may be reproduced, stored in a retrieval system, or transmitted by any means <u>without</u> the written permission of the author.

ISBN-13: 978-1537010540

Printed in the United States of America

All Scripture quotations deliberately taken from the Authorized Version of the Holy Bible, the King James Version.

Cover design by Bill Wegener of
www.ColorEnlargement.com

Do you desire to learn God's Word? Let's grow in His grace together. To begin receiving the *Moments with My Master* email that is sent out two to three times weekly, go to SafeGuardYourSoul.com and sign up. Or, email info@safeguardyoursoul.com.

Victorious Spiritual Survival and

Soul Harvest in these Last Days

Acknowledgments

The LORD be thanked for all the friends, members of Christ's body, He has brought together to complete this volume. Those friends include and yet are not limited to ….

Debbie Lord, Lisa Seiler, Travis Bryan III, Mark Owen, Charles and Sherry Manspeaker, Bill Wegener, Gayle Patton, Darlene Troxler, and BJ Sullivan.

On Style...

❦

Feeding Jesus' beloved sheep requires instilling His truth into hearts. In accordance with this guiding principle, there will be no hesitation to restate Bible verses to teach by repetition and association. This is because there are different occasions where the same verse or passage applies and it is appropriate to show the practical application of His Word as it applies in a variety of situations. The apostle Peter spoke about bringing us into remembrance of the truths of the LORD (2 Peter 1:12, 13, 15; 3:1).

The wisdom of God says, **"He taught me also, and said unto me, Let thine heart retain my words: keep my commandments, and live."** (Proverbs 4:4)

"Give glory to the LORD your God, before he cause darkness, and before your feet stumble upon the dark mountains, and, while ye look for light, he turn it into the shadow of death, and make it gross darkness." Jeremiah 13:16

"Then Jesus said unto them, Yet a little while is the light with you. Walk while ye have the light, lest darkness come upon you: for he that walketh in darkness knoweth not whither he goeth." John 12:35

"I must work the works of him that sent me, while it is day: the night cometh, when no man can work." John 9:4

Table of Contents

Chapter 1
Gross Darkness Shall Cover the Earth 1

Chapter 2
A Time of Trouble 17

Chapter 3
Revelation Bombshell! 35

Chapter 4
Planted in the House of the LORD 57

Chapter 5
Christ's Light is Shining Bright! 71

Chapter 6
Ready or Not – Jesus is Coming! 89

Chapter 7
Get Ready for Warfare....................................107

Chapter 8
Mary Moments in a Martha World...................121

Chapter 9
Narrow is the Way ……..……………..……………133

Chapter 10
What to Do if You Sin…………………..……...……145

Chapter 11
Treasures in Heaven ……………………………….171

Chapter 12
Be Thou Faithful unto Death …………..………...…187

Chapter 13
Don't Miss this Divine
Prescription for Blessing…………………….…..….209

Addendum
Making Peace with God ……………..….…………221

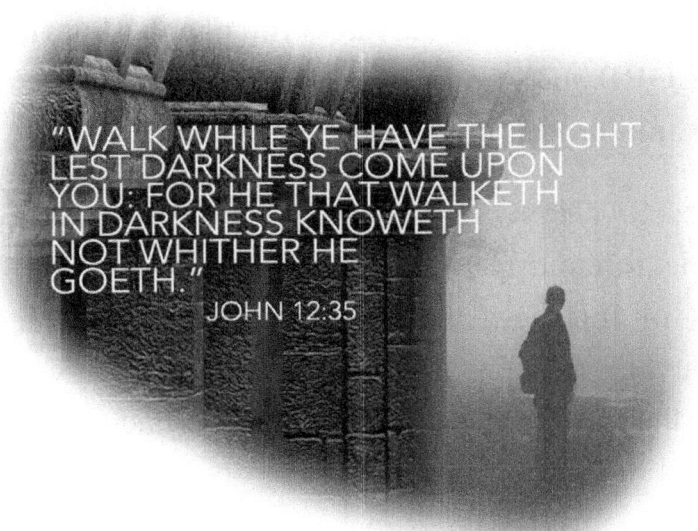

Chapter 1

☙

Gross Darkness ...
Shall Cover the Earth

> "For, behold, the darkness shall cover the
> earth, and gross darkness the people: but the
> LORD shall arise upon thee, and his glory
> shall be seen upon thee." Isaiah 60:2

SAINTS, THINGS ARE GETTING EXCITING! Just as was foretold in Holy Scripture concerning the final days of this age, we are now beholding epidemic, worldwide, rebellion that is sweeping up every single soul that is not firmly rooted and grounded in Jesus Christ!

Jesus is coming.

> "And when these things begin to come to
> pass, then look up, and lift up your heads;
> for your redemption draweth nigh."
> Luke 21:28

May God bless His beloved blood-bought body to be His light and shine the light of Christ into the darkness of this fallen world in this late hour.

As the light of the world – Jesus Christ – is shown into the darkened, desperate hearts of men, many will be saved and forgiven by Jesus' blood!

> "Ye are the salt of the earth: but if the salt
> have lost his savour, wherewith shall it be

> salted? it is thenceforth good for nothing, but to be cast out, and to be trodden under foot of men. ¹⁴ **Ye are the light of the world. A city that is set on an hill cannot be hid.** ¹⁵ **Neither do men light a candle, and put it under a bushel, but on a candlestick; and it giveth light unto all that are in the house.** ¹⁶ **Let your light so shine before men, that they may see your good works, and glorify your Father which is in heaven."**
> **Matthew 5:13-16**

Jesus came to the earth to rescue the perishing. Listen to the Lamb of God ...

> **"To open their eyes, and to turn them from darkness to light, and from the power of Satan unto God, that they may receive forgiveness of sins, and inheritance among them which are sanctified by faith that is in me." Acts 26:18**

Avoiding the End Time Pitfalls

An eerie blanket of darkness looms over all the earth as the end of this age draws ever so near where the dawning of a new Day is upon us. It's a thrilling time for those who are engaged and live in fervent

Nightfall

expectation for their returning Bridegroom of redemption.

> **"And we know that we are of God, and the whole world lieth in wickedness."**
> **1 John 5:19**

During the plagues God sent in the days of Israel's captivity in Egypt, there was darkness for the Egyptians (represents the world's people) and light for the LORD's people (Exodus 7-11). We see this phenomenon throughout History. The Egyptians represented the world, and there was a plague of darkness blanketing Egypt, with the exception of Goshen, where the LORD's people lived. There was light there.

> **"And the LORD said unto Moses, Stretch out thine hand toward heaven, that there may be darkness over the land of Egypt, even darkness which may be felt. ²² And Moses stretched forth his hand toward heaven; and <u>there was a thick darkness in all the land of Egypt three days</u>: ²³ They saw not one another, neither rose any from his place for three days: <u>but all the children of Israel had light in their dwellings</u>."**
> **Exodus 10:21-23**

Ye, Brethren, Are Not in Darkness

"But of the times and the seasons, brethren, ye have no need that I write unto you. 2 For yourselves know perfectly that the day of the Lord so cometh as a thief in the night. 3 For when they shall say, Peace and safety; then sudden destruction cometh upon them, as travail upon a woman with child; and they shall not escape. 4 But ye, brethren, are not in darkness, that that day should overtake you as a thief. 5 Ye are all the children of light, and the children of the day: we are not of the night, nor of darkness. 6 Therefore let us not sleep, as do others; but let us watch and be sober. 7 For they that sleep sleep in the night; and they that be drunken are drunken in the night. 8 But let us, who are of the day, be sober, putting on the breastplate of faith and love; and for an helmet, the hope of salvation. 9 For God hath not appointed us to wrath, but to obtain salvation by our Lord Jesus Christ, 10 Who died for us, that, whether we wake or sleep, we should live together with him. 11 Wherefore comfort yourselves together, and edify one another, even as also ye do." 1 Thessalonians 5:1-11

Nightfall

The righteous have the light of Christ even though we may at times **"walk through the valley of death."** However, fear and trepidation will be upon all who do not know the Good Shepherd (Psalms 23; 91).

> **"And the kings of the earth, and the great men, and the rich men, and the chief captains, and the mighty men, and every bondman, and every free man, hid themselves in the dens and in the rocks of the mountains; [16] And said to the mountains and rocks, Fall on us, and hide us from the face of him that sitteth on the throne, and from the wrath of the Lamb: [17] For the great day of his wrath is come; and who shall be able to stand?" Revelation 6:15-17**

Storm clouds loom in eager expectation for these, **"the days of vengeance"** where the LORD pours out His indignation upon fallen, unrepentant mankind (Luke 21:22).

> **"For the earnest expectation of the creature waiteth for the manifestation of the sons of God. [20] For the creature was made subject to vanity, not willingly, but by reason of him who hath subjected the same in hope, [21] Because the creature itself also shall be**

delivered from the bondage of corruption into the glorious liberty of the children of God. ²² For we know that the whole creation groaneth and travaileth in pain together until now. ²³ And not only they, but ourselves also, which have the firstfruits of the Spirit, even we ourselves groan within ourselves, waiting for the adoption, to wit, the redemption of our body." Romans 8:19-23**

Of these final days before His soon return, Jesus says:

"For these be the days of vengeance, that all things which are written may be fulfilled." Luke 21:22

Heaven's King will soon come back, riding on a white horse. He will battle the armies of the wicked one and will overcome them. Armageddon will be unprecedented. It will be the most horrid event in all of human history. The vengeance of our God shall be poured out without measure.

"And to you who are troubled rest with us, when the Lord Jesus shall be revealed from heaven with his mighty angels, ⁸ In flaming fire taking vengeance on them that know not God, and that obey not the gospel of our

**Lord Jesus Christ: ⁹ Who shall be punished with everlasting destruction from the presence of the Lord, and from the glory of his power; ¹⁰ When he shall come to be glorified in his saints, and to be admired in all them that believe (because our testimony among you was believed) in that day."
2 Thessalonians 1:7-10**

There's going to be a complete restoration of His earth but not till there's a violent war and unparalleled damage, suffering, and bloodshed as fallen man foolishly seeks to battle his Maker.

"But the day of the Lord will come as a thief in the night; in the which the heavens shall pass away with a great noise, and the elements shall melt with fervent heat, the earth also and the works that are therein shall be burned up. ¹¹ Seeing then that all these things shall be dissolved, what manner of persons ought ye to be in all holy conversation and godliness, ¹² Looking for and hasting unto the coming of the day of God, wherein the heavens being on fire shall be dissolved, and the elements shall melt with fervent heat? ¹³ Nevertheless we,

> **according to his promise, look for new heavens and a new earth, wherein dwelleth righteousness. [14] Wherefore, beloved, seeing that ye look for such things, be diligent that ye may be found of him in peace, without spot, and blameless." 2 Peter 3:10-14**

Of our LORD's return, the Bible foretells that He's coming back to punish the wicked – both those who once knew Him and yet have fallen away and those who have rejected His offer to come and freely receive of His offer of salvation.

> **"In flaming fire taking vengeance on them that know not God, and that obey not the gospel of our Lord Jesus Christ."**
> **2 Thessalonians 1:8**

The LORD is going to soon return with a fury to decimate and bring to utter desolation all rebels. Here's the news before the news as reported by the prophet Isaiah:

> **"I have commanded my sanctified ones, I have also called my mighty ones for mine anger, even <u>them that rejoice in my highness</u>. [4] The noise of a multitude in the mountains, like as of a great people; a**

Nightfall

tumultuous noise of the kingdoms of nations gathered together: the LORD of hosts mustereth the host of the battle. ⁵ They come from a far country, from the end of heaven, even the LORD, and the weapons of his indignation, to destroy the whole land. ⁶ Howl ye; for the day of the LORD is at hand; it shall come as a destruction from the Almighty. ⁷ Therefore shall all hands be faint, and every man's heart shall melt: ⁸ And they shall be afraid: pangs and sorrows shall take hold of them; they shall be in pain as a woman that travaileth: they shall be amazed one at another; their faces shall be as flames. ⁹ <u>Behold, the day of the LORD cometh, cruel both with wrath and fierce anger, to lay the land desolate: and he shall destroy the sinners thereof out of it.</u> ¹⁰ For the stars of heaven and the constellations thereof shall not give their light: the sun shall be darkened in his going forth, and the moon shall not cause her light to shine. ¹¹ <u>And I will punish the world for their evil, and the wicked for their iniquity; and I will cause the arrogancy of the proud to cease, and will lay low the haughtiness of the terrible.</u> ¹² I will make a man more

> **precious than fine gold (justice restored); even a man than the golden wedge of Ophir. [13] Therefore I will shake the heavens, and the earth shall remove out of her place, in the wrath of the LORD of hosts, and in the day of his fierce anger." Isaiah 13:3-13**

The battle of the ages awaits the appointed time of the Creator and Judge who will soon reclaim His earth/fallen planet. Multitudes are in the valley of decision while many of those who are supposed to be waiting for the Bridegroom to return are either running low on oil or are completely drained of it (Joel 3:14). They are woefully **"at ease in Zion"** which means they are not **"sober"** and **"vigilant,"** watching and praying to overcome temptation so they **"may be accounted worthy to escape all these things that shall come to pass, and to stand before the Son of man."** (Amos 6:1; 1 Peter 5:8)

In one of the most grave warning passages in all the New Testament, the Son of God alerts us:

> **"And take heed to yourselves, lest at any time your hearts be overcharged with surfeiting, and drunkenness, and cares of this life, and so that day come upon you unawares. [35] For as a snare shall it come on**

all them that dwell on the face of the whole earth. ³⁶ Watch ye therefore, and pray always, that ye may be accounted worthy to escape all these things that shall come to pass, and to stand before the Son of man." Luke 21:34-36

Why such a warning if all who had ever been saved by the Bridegroom were automatically going to make it to the eternal bride chamber? What need would there be for the very Alpha and Omega Himself to issue such a warning if His people were not required by Him to overcome, to remain in love and in close fellowship with Him? This and a myriad of other solemn warnings in the New Testament make it more than abundantly clear that there is great jeopardy of soul in this last hour and that many who once began with Christ, will not end up with Him.

The thought of being deceived should deeply concern and frighten us.

> **"There is a generation that are pure in their own eyes, and yet is not washed from their filthiness." Proverbs 30:12**

> **"There is a way which seemeth right unto a man, but the end thereof are the ways of death." Proverbs 14:12**

Many will be caught off guard at the end with no chance of escape from the divine judgment coming to all who are not with Christ.

> **"He that is not with me is against me; and he that gathereth not with me scattereth abroad." Matthew 12:30**

Do you have the desire to be authentic – to be a genuine disciple of Jesus Christ?

To those who sense the drawing to repentance, harden not your hearts but rather hearken to the call of God before it's too late. Hasten to the foot of the cross where Jesus bled to redeem you.

> **"Wash you, make you clean; put away the evil of your doings from before mine eyes; cease to do evil; ¹⁷ Learn to do well; seek judgment, relieve the oppressed, judge the fatherless, plead for the widow. ¹⁸ Come now, and let us reason together, saith the LORD: though your sins be as scarlet, they shall be as white as snow; though they be red like crimson, they shall be as wool. ¹⁹ If ye be willing and obedient, ye shall eat the good of**

Nightfall

the land: [20] But if ye refuse and rebel, ye shall be devoured with the sword: for the mouth of the LORD hath spoken it."
Isaiah 1:16-20

Victory in "a Time of Trouble"

Biblical Prescription for a Powerful Day in Christ!

Begin with personal identification with Christ in His death so that He can raise you upward for His glory – in His resurrection life and power (Romans 6:3-4; 1 Corinthians 15:1-4; John 3:30; Luke 9:23-24; Colossians 3:3; 2 Corinthians 4:10-12). This is the Gospel as it applies to your daily life with Jesus and this will never change (Romans 6:3-4; 2 Corinthians 4:10-12). Lay it all down in surrender at His feet and He will resurrect your life in His grace to glorify Himself in and through you!

Prayerfully read these following passages in private intimate morning fellowship with the LORD. Your daily life will be greatly enriched and increased in the fellowship and victory of Christ!

   1. Colossians 3:1-4
   2. Philippians 2:3-5
   3. 1 Corinthians 13

Prayer: *Holy Father, I have sinned against You in many ways. You are Holy and I have been unholy. Yet, at this moment – right now if never before – I cry out to Thee LORD, and ask You to forgive my rebellion against You and to wash away all my sins in the blood of Jesus Christ. LORD Jesus, take over my life at this moment and from here forward, You are my LORD, Master, and Savior. Into Your hands I release my spirit, soul, and body. I'm all Yours and You are all mine. I love you LORD Jesus. In Jesus' name, amen.*

CAPTURE POINTS

- For fear of what's coming on the earth, what shall be the reaction of those who are not in the LORD's kingdom? Revelation 6:15-17

- Write Luke 21:34-36 on an index card. Discuss.

- Meditate upon and discuss Proverbs 14:12 and how it can apply to us. Consider how easy it is to be misled and deceived and what the answer to walking in His light is (1 John 1:7, 9; Revelation 3:14-22).

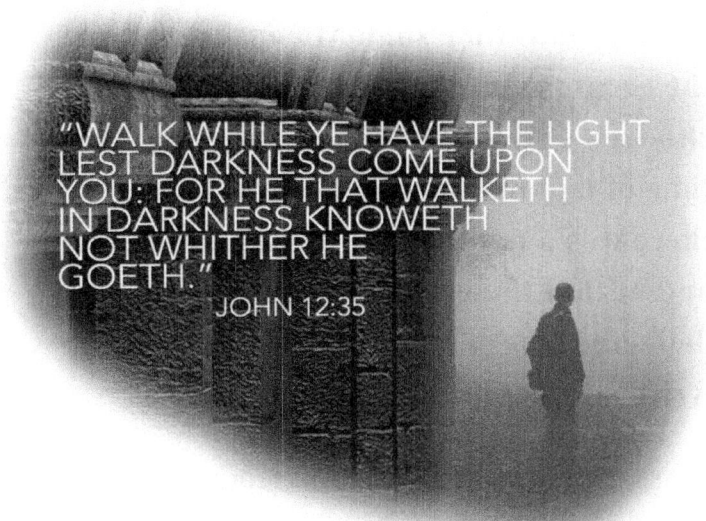

"WALK WHILE YE HAVE THE LIGHT LEST DARKNESS COME UPON YOU: FOR HE THAT WALKETH IN DARKNESS KNOWETH NOT WHITHER HE GOETH."
JOHN 12:35

Chapter 2

☙

A Time of Trouble

> "And at that time shall Michael stand up, the great prince which standeth for the children of thy people: and there shall be a time of trouble, such as never was since there was a nation even to that same time: and at that time thy people shall be delivered, every one that shall be found written in the book." Daniel 12:1

Darkness is descending. Are you ready?

Here Daniel writes:

> "There shall be A TIME OF TROUBLE, such as never was since there was a nation even to that same time: and at that time thy people shall be delivered, every one that shall be found written in the book."
> Daniel 12:1

Christ's true followers will be kept safe, even if they are martyred. In fact, the true followers of Christ who die during this time, will be forever safe in the presence of the Almighty, never to experience any iota of negativity of any kind again (Revelation 21:4).

> "For God hath not appointed us to wrath, but to obtain salvation by our Lord Jesus

> **Christ, [10] Who died for us, that, whether we wake or sleep, we should live together with him. [11] Wherefore comfort yourselves together, and edify one another, even as also ye do." 1 Thessalonians 4:9-11**

The LORD preserved Lot in the midst of a wicked generation of men.

> **"And delivered just Lot, vexed with the filthy conversation of the wicked: [8] (For that righteous man dwelling among them, in seeing and hearing, vexed his righteous soul from day to day with their unlawful deeds;) [9] The Lord knoweth how to deliver the godly out of temptations, and to reserve the unjust unto the day of judgment to be punished." 2 Peter 2:7-9**

> **"For then shall be great tribulation, such as was not since the beginning of the world to this time, no, nor ever shall be." Matthew 24:21**

The hour draws ever so near for the most dangerous and perilous times in human history as told by Daniel the prophet and the LORD Jesus Christ. An hour of such epidemic wickedness has never been known to mankind. Not only natural calamities but more treacherously a time of sinful depravity among men such as has never been manifested in world history.

Matthew 24 is one of the most, if not *the* most significant portions of Holy Scripture concerning the final days of this age.

Matthew 24

"And Jesus went out, and departed from the temple: and his disciples came to him for to shew him the buildings of the temple. ² And Jesus said unto them, See ye not all these things? verily I say unto you, There shall not be left here one stone upon another, that shall not be thrown down. ³ And as he sat upon the mount of Olives, the disciples came unto him privately, saying, Tell us, when shall these things be? and what shall be the sign of thy coming, and of the end of the world? ⁴ And Jesus answered and said unto them, Take heed that no man deceive you. ⁵ For many shall come in my name, saying, I am Christ; and shall deceive many. ⁶ And ye shall hear of wars and rumours of wars: see that ye be not troubled: for all these things must come to pass, but the end is not yet. ^{7} For nation shall rise against nation, and kingdom against kingdom: and there shall be famines, and pestilences, and earthquakes, in divers places. ^{8} All these are the beginning of sorrows. ^{9} Then shall they deliver you up to be afflicted, and shall kill you: and ye shall be hated of all nations for my name's sake. ^{10} And then shall many be offended, and shall betray one another, and shall hate one another. ^{11} And many false prophets shall rise, and shall deceive many. ^{12} And because iniquity shall abound, the love of many shall wax cold. ^{13} But he that shall endure unto the end, the same shall be saved. ^{14} And this gospel of the kingdom shall be preached in all the world for a witness unto all nations; and then shall the end come. ^{15} When ye therefore shall see the abomination of desolation, spoken of by Daniel the prophet, stand in the holy place, (whoso readeth, let him understand:) ^{16} Then let them which be in Judaea flee into the mountains: ^{17} Let him which is on the housetop not come down to take any thing out of his house: ^{18} Neither let him which is in the field return back to take his clothes.

Nightfall

[19] And woe unto them that are with child, and to them that give suck in those days! [20] But pray ye that your flight be not in the winter, neither on the sabbath day: [21] <u>For then shall be great tribulation, such as was not since the beginning of the world to this time, no, nor ever shall be.</u> [22] And except those days should be shortened, there should no flesh be saved: but for the elect's sake those days shall be shortened. [23] Then if any man shall say unto you, Lo, here is Christ, or there; believe it not. [24] For there shall arise false Christs, and false prophets, and shall shew great signs and wonders; insomuch that, if it were possible, they shall deceive the very elect. [25] Behold, I have told you before. [26] Wherefore if they shall say unto you, Behold, he is in the desert; go not forth: behold, he is in the secret chambers; believe it not. [27] For as the lightning cometh out of the east, and shineth even unto the west; so shall also the coming of the Son of man be. [28] For wheresoever the carcase is, there will the eagles be gathered together.
[29] Immediately after the tribulation of those days shall the sun be darkened, and the moon shall not give her light, and the stars

shall fall from heaven, and the powers of the heavens shall be shaken: [30] And then shall appear the sign of the Son of man in heaven: and then shall all the tribes of the earth mourn, and they shall see the Son of man coming in the clouds of heaven with power and great glory. [31] And he shall send his angels with a great sound of a trumpet, and they shall gather together his elect from the four winds, from one end of heaven to the other. [32] Now learn a parable of the fig tree; When his branch is yet tender, and putteth forth leaves, ye know that summer is nigh: [33] So likewise ye, when ye shall see all these things, know that it is near, even at the doors. [34] Verily I say unto you, This generation shall not pass, till all these things be fulfilled. [35] Heaven and earth shall pass away, but my words shall not pass away. [36] But of that day and hour knoweth no man, no, not the angels of heaven, but my Father only. [37] But as the days of Noe were, so shall also the coming of the Son of man be. [38] For as in the days that were before the flood they were eating and drinking, marrying and giving in marriage, until the day that Noe entered into the ark, [39] And knew not until

Nightfall

the flood came, and took them all away; so shall also the coming of the Son of man be. [40] Then shall two be in the field; the one shall be taken, and the other left. [41] Two women shall be grinding at the mill; the one shall be taken, and the other left. [42] Watch therefore: for ye know not what hour your Lord doth come. [43] But know this, that if the goodman of the house had known in what watch the thief would come, he would have watched, and would not have suffered his house to be broken up. [44] Therefore be ye also ready: for in such an hour as ye think not the Son of man cometh. [45] Who then is a faithful and wise servant, whom his lord hath made ruler over his household, to give them meat in due season? [46] Blessed is that servant, whom his lord when he cometh shall find so doing. [47] Verily I say unto you, That he shall make him ruler over all his goods. [48] But and if that evil servant shall say in his heart, My lord delayeth his coming; [49] And shall begin to smite his fellow servants, and to eat and drink with the drunken; [50] The lord of that servant shall come in a day when he looketh not for him, and in an hour that he is not aware of, [51] And shall cut him asunder, and

appoint him his portion with the hypocrites: there shall be weeping and gnashing of teeth."

In this **"time of trouble,"** one of the most insidious, trepidatious, and evil elements will be that many will become **"traitors."** (2 Timothy 3:4) Note above that in verse 48-49 we read of those who will say in their hearts that the LORD delays His coming and so they will cease to continue to vigilantly watch and pray and to remain ready. This includes walking in God's love toward His beloved people (1 John 4:7-8). As a result of this departure from the faith, some will begin to mistreat God's children and that's paramount to mistreating Jesus who says, **"Inasmuch as ye have done it unto one of the least of these my brethren, ye have done it unto me."** (Matthew 25:40) This is clearly speaking of back sliders and not the lost souls who've never been saved. These are **"evil servant(s)"** which means they are part of the **"household."** (v45) The way we treat others, especially the LORD's children, *is* the way we are treating Him.

In the earlier verses of this discourse on the final days of this age, Christ speaks of betrayal when He exclaims:

Nightfall

> "And then shall many be offended, and shall betray one another, and shall hate one another. [11] And many false prophets shall rise, and shall deceive many. [12] And because iniquity shall abound, the love of many shall wax cold. [13] But he that shall endure unto the end, the same shall be saved."
> **Matthew 24:10-13**

Note that because evil will exponentially increase as the day of Christ's return nears, that **"iniquity shall abound (be rampant),"** and that **"the love of many shall wax cold."** The fact that their love for Christ and His children waxes cold clearly indicates that they were once part of His kingdom and that their love was at one time hot. To **"wax cold"** suggests that the temperature of their love for Him descended from a warmer state to a place of coldness. They were once on fire for Jesus. There would be no use for such language if the love of those who had waxed cold hadn't at one time burned hot for Christ.

Beware of Hypocrisy

The LORD is calling you to get all the logs out of your own eye before He can possibly use you (if He so chooses) to help and not condemn others. The LORD would despise the operation of the sin-filled, unrepentant heart that pretends to have His answer for others when you have not sought firstly and continually applied the answer of His Word to yourself. Until you have obeyed God in the very simple things like studying His Word daily and seeking His face daily in holy prayer communion and ministering His Word daily to others, you are still a baby (if even saved) and have no business trying to correct anyone else. If you dare attempt such, Jesus rebukes you as a **"hypocrite"** (Matthew 7:1-5). If you haven't obeyed Christ by ministering His Word to others, especially for a long season or seasons of suffering, you have no idea what being persecuted is like and are a novice at best (or unsaved). This means that you are not spiritually mature and unfit, unqualified to seek to correct and administer restoration to others. God wants you tending to your own heart and the great need you have for personal repentance, brokenness, and dying to self. He would never violate (contradict) His own Word by sending you to correct anyone since you are not qualified (Galatians 6:1-2; Matthew 7:1-5, etc.).

It is quite interesting to see that some among us who have never been in a battle and therefore have no battle scars, find it easy to shoot out foolish words of great arrogance concerning others who are actually in full motion serving Christ (2 Timothy 2:1-4). It's quite amazing how some who have never led one soul to Jesus because they are not obeying Christ's Great Commission command, take up condemnation upon others who are busy about the LORD's work. These I speak of have never fed the Word of God to other believers, yet seem to think they have the answers for those who preach God's Word unrelentingly (Romans 2:10-3). Utter hypocrisy. They have never corrected their own lives and yet foolishly believe God is contradicting His own Word to send them to correct others, which is impossible (Matthew 7:1-5; Galatians 6:1-2). God is calling for repentance and for you to cry out in desperation for Him to break you to the core of your being. Correction – are you qualified to correct?

False Prophets During This "Time of Trouble"

Another element to behold in this glorious revelation of the swiftly approaching finality of all things is the repeated sign of the **"many false prophets"** who will deceive **"many"** not a few. This warning is given to us by the Son of God in the beginning of His answer to the question of when the end would be, and then twice more.

> "The disciples came unto him privately, saying, Tell us, when shall these things be? and what shall be the sign of thy coming, and of the end of the world? ⁴ And Jesus answered and said unto them, Take heed that no man deceive you. ⁵ For many shall come in my name, saying, I am Christ; and shall deceive many... ¹¹ And many false prophets shall rise, and shall deceive many ..." **Matthew 24:3-5, 11**

The **"fruit"** of **"false prophets"** is how Jesus says to identify them. Loving God and walking in His love toward others in this **"time of trouble"** is being learned by His true remnant in this hour. Let's listen to Jesus:

> "Therefore all things whatsoever ye would that men should do to you, do ye even so to them: for this is the law and the prophets. ¹³ Enter ye in at the strait gate: for wide is the gate, and broad is the way, that leadeth to destruction, and many there be which go in thereat: ¹⁴ Because strait is the gate, and narrow is the way, which leadeth unto life, and few there be that find it. ¹⁵ Beware of false prophets, which come to you in sheep's

clothing, but inwardly they are ravening wolves. [16] Ye shall know them by their fruits. Do men gather grapes of thorns, or figs of thistles? [17] Even so every good tree bringeth forth good fruit; but a corrupt tree bringeth forth evil fruit. [18] A good tree cannot bring forth evil fruit, neither can a corrupt tree bring forth good fruit. [19] Every tree that bringeth not forth good fruit is hewn down, and cast into the fire. [20] Wherefore by their fruits ye shall know them." Matthew 7:12-20

The Wise Shall Understand

The wise fear God and are therefore possessed with an eternal perspective. They rejoice to know they will be raised up eternally with the Father and Christ.

"And many of them that sleep in the dust of the earth shall awake, some to everlasting life, and some to shame and everlasting contempt. [3] And they that be wise shall shine as the brightness of the firmament; and they that turn many to righteousness as the stars for ever and ever. [4] But thou, O Daniel, shut up the words, and seal the book, even to the time of the end: many shall run to and fro, and knowledge shall be increased. [5] Then I

Daniel looked, and, behold, there stood other two, the one on this side of the bank of the river, and the other on that side of the bank of the river. ⁶ And one said to the man clothed in linen, which was upon the waters of the river, How long shall it be to the end of these wonders? ⁷ And I heard the man clothed in linen, which was upon the waters of the river, when he held up his right hand and his left hand unto heaven, and sware by him that liveth for ever that it shall be for a time, times, and an half; and when he shall have accomplished to scatter the power of the holy people, all these things shall be finished. ⁸ And I heard, but I understood not: then said I, O my Lord, what shall be the end of these things? ⁹ And he said, Go thy way, Daniel: for the words are closed up and sealed till the time of the end. ¹⁰ Many shall be purified, and made white, and tried; but the wicked shall do wickedly: and <u>none of the wicked shall understand</u>; <u>but the wise shall understand.</u>" Daniel 12:2-10

The righteous have the Holy Spirit in their hearts and hear **"what the Spirit saith unto the churches"** (Revelation 2-3). So they are not in the dark about the

Nightfall

end of all things as we know them on this earth. Yet, the wicked will not know that they are on the verge of eternal incarceration in the flaming pit of condemnation.

1 Thessalonians 5

"But of the times and the seasons, brethren, ye have no need that I write unto you. ² For yourselves know perfectly that the day of the Lord so cometh as a thief in the night. ³ For when they shall say, Peace and safety; then sudden destruction cometh upon them, as travail upon a woman with child; and they shall not escape. ⁴ But ye, brethren, are not in darkness, that that day should overtake you as a thief. ⁵ Ye are all the children of light, and the children of the day: we are not of the night, nor of darkness. ⁶ Therefore let us not sleep, as do others; but let us watch and be sober. ⁷ For they that sleep sleep in the night; and they that be drunken are drunken in the night. ⁸ But let us, who are of the day, be sober, putting on the breastplate of faith and love; and for an helmet, the hope of salvation. ⁹ For God hath not appointed us to wrath, but to obtain salvation by our Lord Jesus Christ, ¹⁰ Who died for us, that, whether we wake or sleep, we should live together with him. [11] Wherefore comfort yourselves together, and edify one another, even as also ye do."

Nightfall

Prayer: *Father, in the name of Jesus, please prepare my heart and life to be ready for this great time of trouble you foretold. Strengthen me in my inner man with your divine power and bless my life to be laid down. Anoint my life with Your Holy Spirit to be dead with Christ. I love You, Jesus. Fill this vessel with Your love for You and others. In Jesus' name, amen.*

CAPTURE POINTS

- Discuss the **"time of trouble"** spoken of by the prophet Daniel and Jesus. See Daniel 12:1 and Matthew 24:21, etc.

- What is the most prevalent sign of the final days of this age? Matthew 24:3-5, 11, 24; 2 Timothy 3:13; 1 John 4:1

- Prayerfully meditate upon and/or discuss how believers can comfort and edify one another in this late hour leading up to Christ's soon return. 1 Thessalonians 5:11 and Hebrews 3:13; 10:24-25.

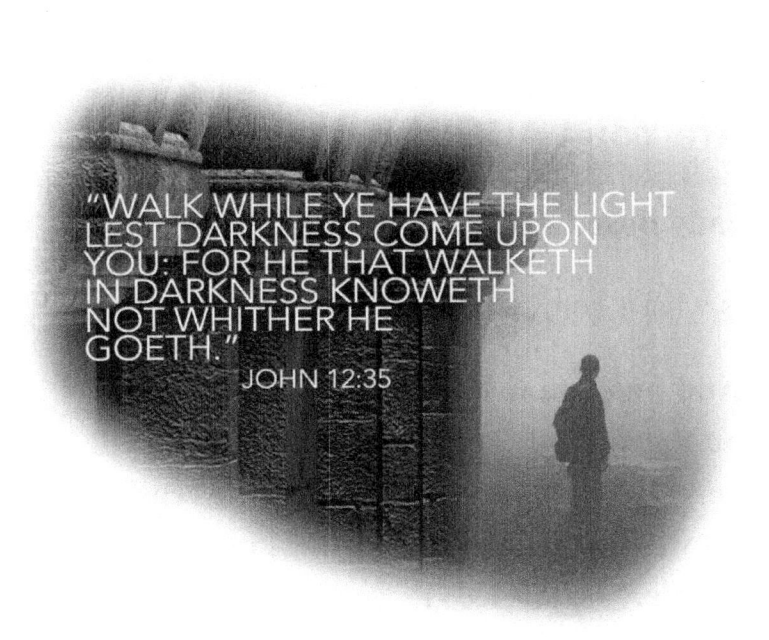

"WALK WHILE YE HAVE THE LIGHT LEST DARKNESS COME UPON YOU: FOR HE THAT WALKETH IN DARKNESS KNOWETH NOT WHITHER HE GOETH."

JOHN 12:35

Chapter 3

☙

Revelation Bombshell!

A Refreshing Biblical Perspective

Of the Last Days

Are You Fretting, Worried, OR Are You LAUGHING?

Biblically Based Apocalyptic Prep

Here's what's coming to this planet…

> **"And I will punish the world for their evil, and the wicked for their iniquity; and I will cause the arrogancy of the proud to cease, and will lay low the haughtiness of the terrible." Isaiah 13:11**

Proper preparation is here. So many are being led astray from what is important to the LORD as He gave us in His Word.

> **"At destruction and famine thou shalt laugh: neither shalt thou be afraid of the beasts of the earth." Job 5:22**

NOT ONLY will Satan not fade away or go away in these final days, his work is increasing as was foretold. AND, the very fact that so many are ignorant of his presence, workings, and devices reveals and confirms the fulfillment of such a prophecy – **"Therefore rejoice, ye heavens, and ye that dwell in them. Woe to the inhabiters of the earth and of the sea! for the**

devil is come down unto you, having great wrath, because he knoweth that he hath but a short time." (Revelation 12:12)

Yet, is God going to stop supplying for and watching over His beloved children just because it's the final days before Christ's soon return and the enemy's work increases? You would think so the way many act with the news of coming doom. Don't worry. Instead, laugh in the joy of Jesus – because He is your Provider and your Protector!

Many worry and fret and fear survival in this fleeting life but the LORD and His apostles had little to say of such, other than to give the many divine promises that God will provide. In fact, concerning the fear of bad things coming soon, Job told us that we should be laughing considering the provision of our loving heavenly Father! (Job 5:22)

Have we been so misguided by the epidemic of wolves who **"mind earthly things"** that we are not about our **"Father's business"** of edifying Jesus' people and, most importantly, winning lost souls? (Luke 2:49; Philippians 3:18-19) Yet, we want to run out and store up food to prepare for what is coming – in this temporary sinful world? Yet, we aren't obeying the Gospel's Great Commission command? How deceived

Nightfall

so many are! Most who claim to know Christ couldn't speak for five minutes about the Great Commission and numerous don't even know what it means! (Matthew 28:18-20; Mark 16:15-20; Luke 24:47-49, The Book of Acts) What astounding delusion and ignorance!

Do you have a full pantry, and yet an empty heart with spotted garments and an empty lamp like the five foolish virgins who were shut out of the eternal kingdom? (Matthew 25:1-13)

Five of Them Were Wise, and Five Were Foolish

> "Then shall the kingdom of heaven be likened unto ten virgins, which took their lamps, and went forth to meet the bridegroom. [2] And <u>five of them were wise, and five were foolish</u>. [3] They that were foolish took their lamps, and took no oil with them: [4] But the wise took oil in their vessels with their lamps. [5] While the bridegroom tarried, they all slumbered and slept. [6] And at midnight there was a cry made, Behold, the bridegroom cometh; go ye out to meet him. [7] Then all those virgins arose, and

trimmed their lamps. ⁸ And the foolish said unto the wise, Give us of your oil; for our lamps are gone out. ⁹ But the wise answered, saying, Not so; lest there be not enough for us and you: but go ye rather to them that sell, and buy for yourselves. ¹⁰ And while they went to buy, the bridegroom came; and they that were ready went in with him to the marriage: and <u>the door was shut</u>.
¹¹ Afterward came also the other virgins, saying, Lord, Lord, open to us. ¹² But he answered and said, Verily I say unto you, I know you not. ¹³ Watch therefore, for ye know neither the day nor the hour wherein the Son of man cometh." Matthew 25:1-13

Notice that the foolish were caught up in the darkness of the day and forfeited eternity in glory. They were irrevocably shut out. The sluggishness and sloth that they allowed to consume their hearts cast them into spiritual lethargy from which they never recovered. Instead of fasting and praying and remaining ready to meet Christ, they indulged in the pleasures of this temporal life and irreversibly lost all which Christ specifically warned against in minute detail (Luke 21:34-36).

Nightfall

"And at midnight there was a cry made, Behold, the bridegroom cometh; go ye out to meet him." (Matthew 25:6) Those who neglected the Bridegroom sought with futility to borrow from the spiritual resources of the wise. God has no grandchildren, only sons and daughters. The LORD makes it clear in His Word that He requires personal responsibility and obedience from each individual. Read Ezekiel 18. Heaven's oil and approval must come firsthand.

Here's one biblical example which informs us that God does not judge us for another person's performance but only for our own:

> **"The soul that sinneth, it shall die. The son shall not bear the iniquity of the father, neither shall the father bear the iniquity of the son: the righteousness of the righteous shall be upon him, and the wickedness of the wicked shall be upon him." Ezekiel 18:20**

Readiness in Light of Christ's Sudden Appearing

> **"Then whosoever heareth the sound of the trumpet, and taketh not warning; if the sword (judgment) come, and take him away, his blood shall be upon his own head.** [5] **He**

heard the sound of the trumpet, and took not warning; his blood shall be upon him. But he that taketh warning shall deliver his soul." Ezekiel 33:4-5

Heaven's Bridegroom is coming suddenly. Are you ready should He come today? Will the door be shut on you? Will you be excluded from His eternal kingdom? Will you miss the marriage supper of the Lamb?

"Behold, I come as a thief. Blessed is he that watcheth, and keepeth his garments, lest he walk naked, and they see his shame." Revelation 16:15

Spiritual preparation trumps physical prep. Where is your heart today? Eternal preparation and remaining **"ready"** hold everlasting consequences and are always the wise choice.

<u>"Be ye therefore ready also: for the Son of man cometh at an hour when ye think not."</u> Luke 12:40

Jesus taught us over and over and over to **"Be ye therefore ready,"** and nothing is more important than simply living **"ready"** to meet Christ because any one of us could pass into eternity today and when our time comes – by His return or our death – if we are abiding holy in Christ, we shall be with Him but if not, we shall suffer **"eternal damnation"** (Matthew 24-25; Mark 3:29; Luke 12:35-40; 1 John 2:28-3:3; Revelation 2-3, etc.). Please keep this in mind precious saints. The LORD has never led me to try to figure out the details of His return, but only to know that it is at hand as a **"thief in the night"** and that He wants me to **"be ready"** (Luke 12:35-40; 1 Thessalonians 5:2; 2 Peter 3:10-17).

Specifically concerning the soon return of the Son of God, the apostle John wrote:

> **"And every man that hath this hope in him purifieth himself, even as he is pure."**
> **1 John 3:3**

The word "prepping" has become a buzz word in our society for those who are preparing for the end of life as we know it. But just WHAT are you prepping for? Are you preparing to be ready to meet Christ?

IF you name Jesus as your LORD and Savior, stop supporting the wolves who refuse to preach the full counsel of God's Word in the holy fear of God! Run for your life! Yea, indeed run for your soul! If the

"Christian" leader is not preparing you to meet Jesus with a pure white garment, you are supporting a wolf!

For exactly what type of people is Jesus soon to return?

> **"Christ also loved the church, and gave himself for it; 26 That he might sanctify and cleanse it with the washing of water by the word, 27 That he might present it to himself a glorious church, not having spot, or wrinkle, or any such thing; but that it should be holy and without blemish." Ephesians 5:25-27**

Be Ye Therefore Ready!

> **"Let your loins be girded about, and your lights burning; 36 And ye yourselves like unto men that wait for their lord, when he will return from the wedding; that when he cometh and knocketh, they may open unto him immediately. 37 Blessed are those servants, whom the lord when he cometh shall find watching: verily I say unto you, that he shall gird himself, and make them to sit down to meat, and will come forth and serve them. 38 And if he shall come in the second watch, or come in the third watch, and find them so, blessed are those servants.**

Nightfall

> [39] And this know, that if the goodman of the house had known what hour the thief would come, he would have watched, and not have suffered his house to be broken through.
> [40] **<u>Be ye therefore ready also: for the Son of man cometh at an hour when ye think not.</u>**"
> **Luke 12:35-40**

Jesus' teachings make it abundantly clear that when one is **"ready"** for Christ's soon return, it will be obvious in that he/she is serving Jesus and others above himself (Philippians 2:3-4).

> **"Let no man seek his own, but every man another's wealth." 1 Corinthians 10:24**

The Son of God exhibited, established and taught that serving Him and others is of the highest priority in His Father's kingdom.

> **"But he that is greatest among you shall be your servant. [12] And whosoever shall exalt himself shall be abased; and he that shall humble himself shall be exalted."**
> **Matthew 23:11-12**

The authentic disciple is crucified with Christ and abandoned to serve the LORD and others

(Matthew 22:37-40). Such a person is being made free by obedience to the truth of the One who is the truth and came to give all for the world so that we could have life.

"Servanthood is the most noble profession of all time as was demonstrated by Christ, our Creator and King. Sadly, precious few are willing to take this course ... Serving Christ and others is pure joy and we can live by it." Eliset Igat

IF YOU are living to serve yourself, you are:

1) not even saved, and

2) fulfilling the prophecy of 2 Timothy 3:1-7.

Any person who is not following Christ by serving God and others before self, is not truly following Jesus and cannot have a clear conscience (1 Timothy 1:5; etc.).

One of the places one's disposition manifests is in relationships. When we walk in love, we are fulfilling God's will in the relationships He blesses us to have – friends or otherwise. The self-loving counterfeit is already or is going to be a nightmare in a friendship or marriage.

Any person who is not learning to humbly serve, is not serving Christ at all. Being possessed by **"the mind of Christ,"** which is a key visible proof of legitimate salvation, is proof (Philippians 2:3-10).

ABS = Always Be Serving – God and others, and not self – is a biblical model for daily living.

Jesus' Specifics on Being "Ready"

> **"And take heed to yourselves, lest at any time your hearts be overcharged with surfeiting (overeating and overindulgence), and drunkenness, and cares of this life (too busy for God), and so that day come upon you unawares. [35] For as a snare (trap) shall it come on all them that dwell on the face of the whole earth. [36] Watch ye therefore, and pray always, that ye may be accounted worthy to escape all these things that shall come to pass, and to stand before the Son of man." Luke 21:34-36**

Are you truly **"ready"** according to Jesus? Are you watching, living a life of prayer communion with the LORD while avoiding the sins of the flesh, including overindulging in this world's goods? Is Christ truly first in your day and life or are you too busy for the LORD?

If you wish to be with Christ eternally instead of Hell, you had better fear this!

> **"And I say unto you my friends, Be not afraid of them that kill the body, and after that have no more that they can do. ⁵ But I will forewarn you whom ye shall fear: Fear him, which after he hath killed hath power to cast into hell; yea, I say unto you, Fear him." Luke 12:4-5**

Are YOU about your **"Father's business"** or have you fallen away and are now lukewarm and ready to be spewed, vomited, rejected? (Revelation 3:15-16) IF you are truly following the only Savior, you are today about HIS business and not your own. If you are not about HIS business, you do not possess saving faith and are deceived.

> **"And he said unto them, How is it that ye sought me? wist (knew) ye not that I must be about <u>my Father's business</u>?" Luke 2:49**

Nightfall

Encouraging Word About These Final Days of History as We Know It

Do You **"love His appearing"?**

Those who are fretting about and running here and there to prepare for these last days and yet are not about the heavenly **"Father's business"** of building up and teaching God's Word and communicating the Gospel to lost souls are in big trouble! They are not prepared to meet Christ who is soon going to return for those who are looking for Him and **"love his appearing."** (2 Timothy 4:8; Hebrews 9:28)

Are You Looking for Him to Return Today?

> **"And as it is appointed unto men once to die, but after this the judgment: [28] So Christ was once offered to bear the sins of many; and unto them that look for him shall he appear the second time without sin unto salvation." Hebrews 9:27-28**

So many are seeking to preserve their own flesh in this temporary world with no regard for eternity. The true remnant disciple is looking to the next world, not this one!

> "Wherefore Jesus also, that he might sanctify the people with his own blood, suffered without the gate. ¹³ Let us go forth therefore unto him without the camp, bearing his reproach. ¹⁴ <u>For here have we no continuing city, but we seek one to come</u>. ¹⁵ By him therefore let us offer the sacrifice of praise to God continually, that is, the fruit of our lips giving thanks to his name."
> **Hebrews 13:12-15**

It would be better to be found of Christ with an empty stomach and your hand to the plow than with creature comforts on this earth and no Christ-magnifying fruit!

> "And Jesus said unto him, No man, having put his hand to the plough, and looking back, is fit for the kingdom of God."
> **Luke 9:62**

Fearing God with Little in This World

> "Better is little with the fear of the Lord than great treasure and trouble therewith."
> **Proverbs 15:16**

A smidgen of dried out food is better than to be out of fellowship with Christ and His people.

Nightfall

> **"Better is a dry morsel, and quietness therewith, than an house full of sacrifices with strife." Proverbs 17:1**

The preparation we need is simply to be steadfast about our Father's business and not to panic or be fearful! That's what Scripture teaches. In fact, the true, abiding disciple can actually **"laugh"** at the thought of **"destruction and famine…"** (Job 5:22) Has God changed? Is the LORD's arm shortened? Has He lost His infinite strength? (Isaiah 59:1-2) We as believers must be passionately spreading this timely message from the ever-relevant Word of God **"which liveth and abideth for ever."** (1 Peter 1:23)

> **"Therefore, my beloved brethren, be ye stedfast, unmoveable, always abounding in the work of the Lord, forasmuch as ye know that your labour is not in vain in the Lord." 1 Corinthians 15:58**

It's clear that those who are busy trying to preserve their lives in this fleeting world are not ready to meet Jesus. Yet, these same professors have no interest in being prepared to meet Christ as a wise virgin disciple. They prove such by their lack of daily attendance to Him. In contrast, the wise virgin saint is daily seeking His face, full of His Word and Spirit, and looking for the soon return of their Bridegroom. Those who choose to neglect the Bridegroom are lost and going to be shut out of the eternal kingdom of God (Matthew 25:1-13).

> **"For if these things be in you, and abound, they make you that ye shall neither be barren nor unfruitful in the knowledge of our Lord Jesus Christ. 9 But he that lacketh these things is blind, and cannot see afar off, and hath forgotten that he was purged from his old sins. 10 Wherefore the rather, brethren, give diligence to make your calling and election sure: for if ye do these things, ye shall never fall: 11 For so an entrance shall be ministered unto you abundantly into the everlasting kingdom of our Lord and Saviour Jesus Christ. 12 Wherefore I will not be negligent to put you always in remembrance of these things, though ye know them, and be established in the present truth. 13 Yea, I think it meet, as long as I am in this tabernacle, to stir you up by putting you in remembrance;" 2 Peter 1:8-13**

Keeping your vessel (heart and mind) full of the oil of His divine Word and Spirit are essential to having an abundant entrance into the Bridal chamber in the end.

Nightfall

"Whosoever shall seek to save his life shall lose it; and whosoever shall lose his life shall preserve it." Luke 17:33

There's No Fear in Those Who Diligently Seek His Holy Face Continually!

"Glory ye in his holy name: let the heart of them rejoice that seek the Lord. [11] Seek the Lord and his strength, seek his face continually." 1 Chronicles 16:10-11

Pucker up!

The purpose of our whole existence, as given by our Creator, is knowing, loving, and worshiping Him (John 17:3; Philippians 3:10). There is no greater purpose or prep one can participate in than getting to know the LORD. The psalmist captures this truth in the 2nd Psalm:

"Serve the Lord with fear, and rejoice with trembling. [12] Kiss the Son, lest he be angry, and ye perish from the way, when his wrath is kindled but a little. Blessed are all they that put their trust in him." Psalms 2:11-12

Memorize This!

> **"But whoso hearkeneth unto me shall dwell safely, and shall be quiet from fear of evil." Proverbs 1:33**

Are you going to **"dwell safely"** eternally?

It's time to sprint to the finish!

> **"Wherefore seeing we also are compassed about with so great a cloud of witnesses, let us lay aside every weight, and the sin which doth so easily beset us, and let us run with patience the race that is set before us, ² Looking unto Jesus the author and finisher of our faith; who for the joy that was set before him endured the cross, despising the shame, and is set down at the right hand of the throne of God. ³ For consider him that endured such contradiction of sinners against himself, lest ye be wearied and faint in your minds." Hebrews 12:1-3**

The Essential Daily Cross Most Pastors Refuse to Teach

Tragically, the modern gospel is not the original Gospel given to us by Christ and His holy apostles. One of the paramount components of the Gospel of

Nightfall

Jesus is the daily cross – the putting under of one's flesh so that Christ alone can reign in our daily lives (Matthew 16:24-25; Luke 9:23-24; John 12:23-25; Romans 6; Galatians 2:20; Colossians 3:3, etc.).

The apostle Paul spoke of keeping his body or flesh subdued. He wrote:

> **"Know ye not that they which run in a race run all, but one receiveth the prize? So run, that ye may obtain.** [25] **And every man that striveth for the mastery is temperate in all things. Now they do it to obtain a corruptible crown; but we an incorruptible.** [26] **I therefore so run, not as uncertainly; so fight I, not as one that beateth the air:** [27] **But I keep under my body, and bring it into subjection: lest that by any means, when I have preached to others, I myself should be a castaway." 1 Corinthians 9:24-27**

It's the exact hour for you to lay down your life without reserve. Fast and pray (Isaiah 58). Cry out to the LORD to unite your heart to fear His holy name (Psalms 86:11). Ask Him to bless you to be anointed to the death and burial of the self-life so that He can raise you upward for His eternal glory alone!

Prayer: *Holy Father, break me to the core of my being! Please Father, in Jesus' name, do this most essential work! Let Thy holy fear fill my innermost being! May Christ alone be glorified in this life You have given. Grant Your Holy Spirit anointing to the burial of the old man that Jesus may be lifted up and glorified in Jesus' name.*

CAPTURE POINTS

- Read and discuss Christ's words of severe warning found in Luke 21:34-36.

- In Psalms 2:11-12, how does Holy Scripture instruct us to serve the LORD? What might God mean when He uses the words **"Kiss the Son"**? Discuss, sticking strictly to Scripture revelation and not just personal feelings.

- Prayerfully read and discuss 1 Corinthians 9:24-27. Suggestion: memorize 1 Corinthians 9:27.

Todd Tomasella

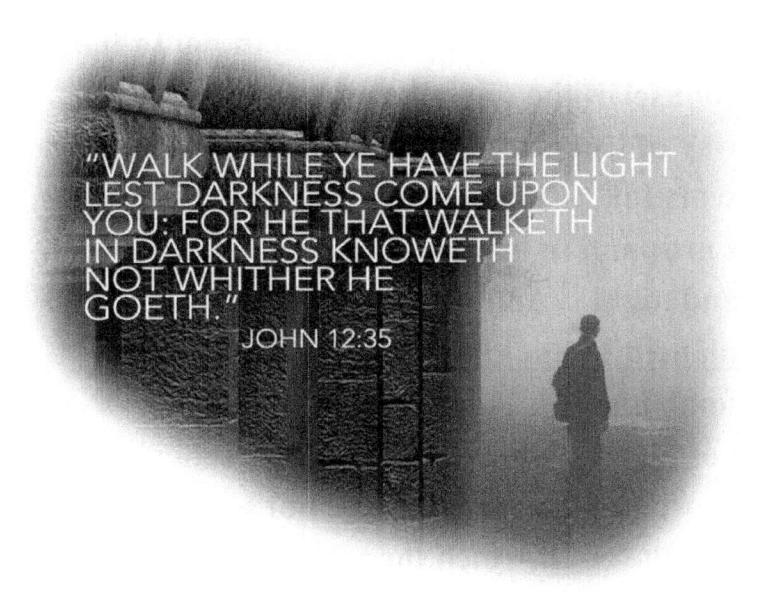

"WALK WHILE YE HAVE THE LIGHT LEST DARKNESS COME UPON YOU: FOR HE THAT WALKETH IN DARKNESS KNOWETH NOT WHITHER HE GOETH."
JOHN 12:35

Chapter 4

☙

Planted in the House of the LORD

Nightfall

**"Blessed *is* the man that walketh not in the counsel of the ungodly, nor standeth in the way of sinners, nor sitteth in the seat of the scornful. ² But his delight *is* in the law of the Lord; and in his law doth he meditate day and night. ³ And he shall be like a tree <u>planted by the rivers of water</u>, that bringeth forth his fruit in his season; his leaf also shall not wither; and whatsoever he doeth shall prosper. ⁴ The ungodly *are* not so: but *are* like the chaff which the wind driveth away. ⁵ Therefore the ungodly shall not stand in the judgment, nor sinners in the congregation of the righteous. ⁶ For the Lord knoweth the way of the righteous: but the way of the ungodly shall perish."
Psalms 1:1-6**

According to Psalms 1, being **"planted by the rivers of water"** guarantees that we are producing good **"fruit."** In fact, as we read this passage, it is a good time for each of us to examine if we are truly producing good fruit. If we are not bearing good fruit, it's due to the absence of a true, abiding relationship with Jesus Christ, the Vine (John 15:1-6, 16). Though fruit saves no one, it's also certain that all who know and are remaining in Christ, are bearing good fruit. The adage is true, "The root determines the fruit" (Romans 11:16; James 3:12).

Lisa Seiler frames it this way:

"Beloved, whether you acknowledge it or not, we are part of a vine – Jesus, 'the vine' (John 15). It is our daily, yea, constant choice to be rooted and grounded in Christ. Such will determine whether we bear fruit that is enhancing His kingdom or doing just the opposite. Our daily choices in the little things will either bear fruit, waste the one thing we can never replace: time; or worst of all, we can bear rotten fruit that harms the kingdom of God and in so doing bring His wrath upon us. It is our calling and duty to examine the fruits of our labors to see if they are indeed good. Satan is cunning and crafty. He often just keeps us 'too busy' to bear fruit."

Being planted in Christ and among His sanctified saints, is essential to flourishing and escaping the judgment destined for **"the ungodly"** (1 Peter 4:18; 2 Peter 2:5-6).

The most luscious greenery can be seen near rivers just as the most healthy, vibrant disciples of Jesus are planted in the rich soil of His presence, His Word, and

Nightfall

fellowship with His saints. How close we remain to Him, the True Vine, is the key to producing good fruit.

> **"Those that be <u>planted in the house (family) of the Lord</u> shall flourish in the courts of our God. ¹⁴ They shall still bring forth fruit in old age; they shall be fat and flourishing;" Psalms 92:13-14**

Bayith is the Hebrew word from which we get **"house"** here and that is important. It means *family*. Yes, *family* – not a physical building or limited to a few Christians who meet at one certain place weekly as if they are a club exclusively reserved for those who have become members of that club. That structure has been set up and is being followed by those leaders who wish to control and to **"make merchandise of you"** using their business model for church (2 Peter 2:1-3). They have basically farmed their communities and cornered their market. Think about that.

God's Word informs us that the blood-bought body of Christ is an eternal **"family."** – **"For this cause I bow my knees unto the Father of our Lord Jesus Christ, ¹⁵ Of whom <u>the whole FAMILY</u> in heaven and earth is named."** (Ephesians 3:14-15)

Does this sound like the modern church with all its emphasis on buildings and physical things? **"For Israel hath forgotten his Maker, and buildeth temples; and Judah hath multiplied fenced cities: but I will send a fire upon his cities, and it shall devour the palaces thereof."** (Hosea 8:14) The true body of Christ is a **"SPIRITUAL house"** or people. 1 Peter 2:5 says **"Ye also, as lively stones, are built up a spiritual house, an holy priesthood, to offer up spiritual sacrifices, acceptable to God by Jesus Christ."**

The modern so-called "church membership" push and coercion is sinful and rebellious and has no reconciliation with New Testament Christianity. No such thing occurred among the earliest disciples. It is a shame that so much time and energy and manipulation is spent by wolves behind pulpits to get people to sign their roll. Especially when so little is being invested in grounding them in the Word of God which is exactly the stated purpose for which God calls men out to serve Him in ministry. Read Ephesians 4:11-15. Beguilers exploit their prey as if all they are is nickels, noses, and numbers.

You see, friend, these enterprising business builders know that if a person signs up to be a member, they

Nightfall

will feel obligated to give their money to that church club. Statistics reveal that this is true and that's what they go by – what makes the most money to pay the mortgage. They are not interested in what God's stated will is.

Being **"planted in the house of the Lord"** does NOT mean being a good church member but rather a fervent follower and worshiper of Jesus Christ, our **"Exceeding great reward."** (Genesis 15:1)

But just what does it mean to be **"planted in the house of the Lord"**? Does that mean finding and joining a church? No. Does that mean being a good church member? No.

Biblically speaking, being **"planted in the house of the Lord"** means abiding richly in Christ and His body in **"daily"** fellowship. Beguiling hirelings have taught us that attending and joining their local church and becoming a member is what being a Christian is all about and yet, such a concept is fully inconsistent with what we read on the pages of the New Testament Scriptures (Acts 2:42-47).

For their own self-serving purposes, deceivers have redefined what it means to walk with Christ in a fruit-bearing, abiding relationship.

The LORD has been very gracious to us. Recently, I read Exodus 17 afresh and was reminded of the great need for fellow brethren in our lives! That is, surrounding ourselves with true believers who will uphold us in prayer and fellowship. This is so that we can mutually be provoking one another to love and good works and growing in God's grace (Hebrews 3:13; 10:24-25; 2 Peter 1:2; 3:18). This is for exhortation, admonition, edification, and at times, loving rebuke (1 Corinthians 14:20; Colossians 3:16; 4:2, 12; 2 Timothy 4:2; Hebrews 3:13; 10:24-25).

> **"But exhort one another <u>daily</u>, while it is called To day; lest any of you be hardened through the deceitfulness of sin. ... And let us consider one another to provoke unto love and to good works: 25 Not forsaking the assembling of ourselves together, as the manner of some is; but exhorting one another: and so much the more, as ye see the day approaching." Hebrews 3:13; 10:24-25**

Considering this passage, many who think they are good due to being a good weekly church member, will not be ready when Christ returns or if their life ends (whichever comes first). They have been grossly misled as to what the Christian life is.

Nightfall

Most pastors read into these passages the idea that you need to join their church and yet such is nowhere to be found in these verses of Holy Writ. They were taught this tradition and it's to their enterprising advantage, yet it's not the New Testament model. The New Testament Scriptures reveal that the body of Christ – the earliest saints being our example and pattern – were a **"daily"** and not a weekly (weakly) church. They met **"house to house daily,"** right? (Acts 2:42-47; 20:20) Jesus taught a **"daily"** following of Him through denial of self, a cross-bearing relationship where we allow Him to reign instead of ourselves and we **"love one another"** as He loves us (Luke 9:23-24; John 13:34-35, etc.). That friends, is being **"planted in the house of the Lord."**

It is telling that the word **"daily"** appears 63 times in God's Word. Christ used the word **"daily"** six of those times concerning His own mission and His mandate upon all who would truly follow Him and not be surprised in the end. Daily fellowship with our heavenly Father, Jesus, and His beloved family is the biblical definition of being **"planted in the house of the Lord."**

Paul wrote his letter to Philemon to **"to the church in thy house."** (Philemon 1:2)

It's interesting to note that the great apostle Paul was not a stage production hireling. He didn't wait till people came to his Saturday or Sunday performance hall so he could entertain them and show them how wonderful he was at delivering the message or staging the event. It's interesting that biblically speaking, a **"hypocrite"** is defined as an *actor* or *poser*. Jesus called false leaders **"hypocrites"** in His day and as Scripture promises us, nothing has changed today (Ecclesiastes 1:9; 2 Timothy 3:13; 1 John 4:1). The Greek word for **"hypocrite"** is *hupokrite* which is defined as an *actor out of an assumed character, stage player, dissembler.* Folks, most meetings in physical church buildings are nothing more than staged productions put on by a committee of clowns or actors. Remember, they have a mortgage to pay and if they tell their audience the hard truths of Scripture, there won't be many patronizing their church business with their attendance and tithes. It's a business model. No doubt about it.

> **"And how I kept back nothing that was profitable unto you, but have shewed you, and have taught you publickly, and from house to house." Acts 20:20**

Paul taught out of his own **"house."**

Nightfall

"And Paul dwelt two whole years in his own hired house, and received all that came in unto him, **[31] Preaching the kingdom of God, and teaching those things which concern the Lord Jesus Christ, with all confidence, no man forbidding him." Acts 28:30-31**

The synagogue was a type of the church building concept of ministry today. When you look up the word **"synagogue"** in the New Testament, in all places that it appears, you may discover a variety of interesting things. You will see that it was a mission field in many cases. It certainly wasn't a fixed place where the saints all met once weekly. No disciple is ever seen inviting someone to "go to church." No, they knew Jesus and were making Him known **"publickly and from house to house"** and **"in the market daily with them that met with him."** (Acts 17:17; 20:20) They **"went every where preaching the word."** (Acts 8:4) You will discover that many of the persecutions against Christ and His disciples came out of those who convened in these synagogues as good "church members" in those so-called "houses of worship."

This is a whole different picture than what we see today in the structure of the apostate, tradition-controlled modern church world where false leaders do not want the individual disciple to learn God's Word and to go **"every where preaching the word."** (Acts 8:4) Why not? – Because then they can't control and **"make merchandise"** of them (2 Peter 2:1-3). They keep the sheep pacified and complacent to exploit them for their own self-serving purposes (Philippians 3:18-19). Again, deceitful hirelings are building a church *business* and are not interested in Christ's *kingdom* being advanced by every member of His body as was being done in the early church (Ephesians 4:11-14). Wolves are not following Christ but rather, are self-willed and given over to their own lusts (Isaiah 56:10-12; Jeremiah 23). They therefore, are not interested in participating in the building of Christ's church.

The bearing of good fruit is the key consistent mark of all who know and remain in Jesus Christ (Matthew 3:10; 7:19; John 15:1-6, 16, etc.).

Below is an example of how Paul and those who were true disciples of Jesus were forced to depart from the rebellious rebels who occupied the "church building," manifesting their **"evil heart(s) of unbelief"** while clinging to their traditions (Hebrews 3:12-14). In a school atmosphere for two years, Paul then taught those who truly knew Jesus and wanted to genuinely follow the Lord.

Nightfall

"And he went into the synagogue (church building), and spake boldly for the space of three months, disputing and persuading the things concerning the kingdom of God. ⁹ But <u>when divers were hardened, and believed not, but spake evil of that way before the multitude, he departed from them, and separated the disciples</u>, disputing daily in the school of one Tyrannus. ¹⁰ And this continued by the space of two years; so that all they which dwelt in Asia heard the word of the Lord Jesus, both Jews and Greeks. ¹¹ And God wrought special miracles by the hands of Paul." Acts 19:8-10

So, where does that leave you? I believe there are some, if not many, reading these words who should follow Paul's example and come out of the church mentality, the church world, and modern church formula and simply follow Christ daily. Yoke up with true disciples who truly walk in the Spirit with Jesus, following Him fervently and daily.

Is the LORD calling you to get a real life with Him?

Beware. Being planted in Christ Jesus is what matters supremely and is of utmost importance. For without this, we have nothing and are Hell bound. Yet, hireling wolves aren't interested in preaching this to you. They want you to be dependent upon them so they can justify their salary and **"make merchandise of you."** (2 Peter 2:1-3) They are using you. That's why they never preach the cross or things that convict you of sin, nor call you to repent and lay down your life to prevent your perishing eternally. If you refuse to truly lay down your life you will perish eternally in the lake of fire (Revelation 2-3; 21:7-8; 27; 22:14-15, etc.).

Nightfall

Prayer: *Dear heavenly Father, please teach me to evaluate every fruit that I bear today and every day. Cause me to be acutely aware of whether or not I am abiding in the True Vine moment-by-moment. Help me to discover and steer clear of those who are not focused on building Your house. Jesus, please bless me to be the kind of believer who provokes others to love and good works. LORD Jesus, please put Your guiding hand heavily upon me and draw me to people and places where I can fellowship with true born-again, abiding believers daily. LORD, please let my life be rooted in You. Fill me afresh with Your Holy Ghost and help me to be fruitful and please You in all my thoughts and actions. In Jesus' precious name, amen.*

CAPTURE POINTS

- Read and discuss the reasons for the fruitfulness of the godly man. Psalms 1:1-3.
- Consider and perhaps discuss the difference between how the earliest believers fellowshipped as contrasted with the practices that can be observed in the modern church world. Acts 2:42-47, etc.
- Read 1 Peter 2:5 and discuss the difference between the **"spiritual house"** of the LORD and mere "church membership" as it's done in the modern church world.

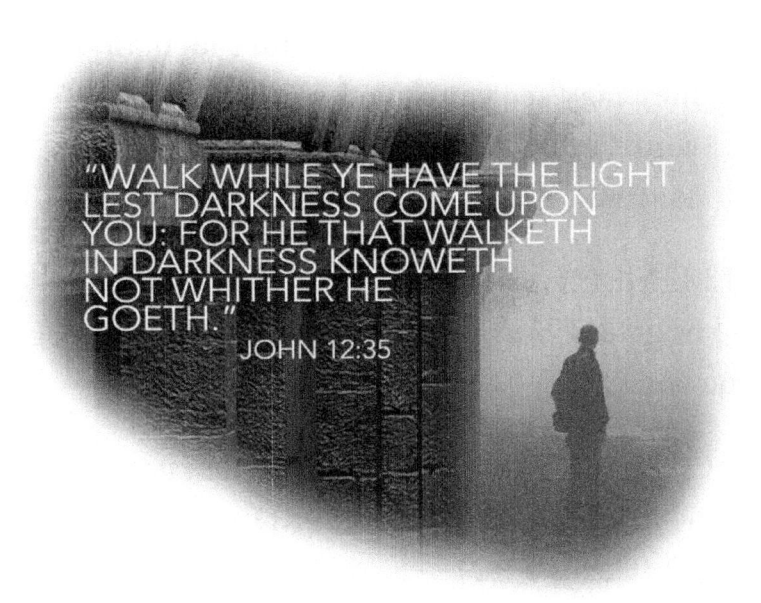

"WALK WHILE YE HAVE THE LIGHT LEST DARKNESS COME UPON YOU: FOR HE THAT WALKETH IN DARKNESS KNOWETH NOT WHITHER HE GOETH."
JOHN 12:35

Chapter 5

☙

Christ's Light is Shining Bright!

Nightfall

"Let your light so shine before men, that they may see your good works, and glorify your Father which is in heaven."
Matthew 5:16

REMEMBER that the darker this fleeting world gets, the brighter Christ's light is going to shine through His true body!

In Genesis 1 where we read that darkness had fallen upon the whole earth, the LORD said **"Let there be light."** (Genesis 1:3)

"And God said, Let there be light: and there was light." Genesis 1:3

In similar fashion and through those whom Jesus says are the conduits of His holy light, the LORD is saying **"Let there be light"** in the darkened hearts of men! And that light of truth is what He shines into their hearts every time He uses one of His saints!

Christ is the great Soul Winner and He is actively using those who are available in this late hour, as darkness blankets the earth preceding His soon return (Matthew 24:10-13; 2 Timothy 3:13, etc.).

Spiritual darkness is increasing and so is the power of Jesus, the Light of the world, to rescue sinners who will otherwise perish.

> **"Wherefore he saith, Awake thou that sleepest, and arise from the dead, and Christ shall give thee light.** [15] **See then that ye walk circumspectly, not as fools, but as wise,** [16] **Redeeming the time, because the days are evil." Ephesians 5:14-16**

As the Holy Spirit foretold, night is falling, moral darkness is descending upon the whole earth in the church, government and secular world. The Great Shepherd of His sheep is orchestrating a harvest of precious souls for whom He came and bled. His **"labourers"** are diligently planting the seed of His Word and will be rewarded for all eternity (Psalms 126:5-6; Matthew 9:35-38; Hebrews 13:20).

Jesus and Janelle

ESTES PARK, Colorado: A precious lady was the glorious focal objective of divine love today in Estes Park, Colorado. As only God could have orchestrated, a lovely lady and I began to talk. Our paths collided and God's Word was discussed and communicated widely with our LORD's anointing/presence. Jesus was

Nightfall

all over it! After about 2-3 hours of delightful conversation, Janelle began suddenly to weep – with tears pouring down her cheeks nonstop for the next 45 minutes. She began confessing to me that she had been considering ending it all due to the hopelessness, troubles, and feelings of uselessness she was facing. She continued to receive our LORD's truth, love, invitation, and exhortation to **"Seek ye first the kingdom of God and his righteousness and ALL these things SHALL be added unto you."** (Matthew 6:33) Also, **"Come unto me, all ye that labour and are heavy laden (guilt, shame, hopelessness), and I will give you rest. ²⁹ Take my yoke upon you, and learn of me; for I am meek and lowly in heart: and ye shall find rest unto your souls. ³⁰ For my yoke is easy, and my burden is light."** (Matthew 11:28-30)

When asked if she were ready to pray and unreservedly turn her life over to the One who gave it, Janelle asked if we could go outside and so we found a nearby bench on the shore of the beautiful river pictured.

Amid the soothing sounds of the flowing river, tears of brokenness and joy continued to flow (like that river) down her cheeks. Janelle was led in a prayer of repentance. She prayed sincerely from her heart as the LORD Jesus took over as the new Master of her life!

Janelle (in her 60's) is a visitor here in Estes Park (on vacation with family members for a short time) and was overwhelmed at how only the LORD could have ordained such an encounter (Romans 8:28-29).

We continued to talk and our LORD's foundation continued to be laid (1 Corinthians 3:11). She asked if I could come have dinner with her and her family and expressed her desire for us all to have a Bible study together!

We are living in Acts 28 saints! Have you read the book of Acts lately?

Please lift up Janelle in prayer according to Philippians 1:6; 2:12-13 and Colossians 4:12.

God's "Good Will"

The Father did not send His only begotten Son to save us just to make us comfortable in this fallen world. No, there are souls He desires to save and just as the LORD used others to plant the seed and lead you to Him, He wants to use you.

"Glory to God in the highest, and on earth peace, good will toward men." Luke 2:14

The ultimate evidence of God's love and **"good will"** – His loving kindness and goodness – toward fallen mankind is that He crucified His Son to save us – **"while we were yet sinners."** (Romans 5:6, 8) The cross is the ultimate expression of love – God's love for mankind. 2 Corinthians 5:19 informs us; **"God was in Christ, reconciling the world unto himself, not imputing their trespasses unto them; and hath committed unto us the word of reconciliation."** (2 Corinthians 5:19) Some would erroneously have you believe that God hates sinners. If that were the case, WHY did He save your own wretched, filthy, sinful, depraved soul, and that He did by crucifying His Son for you? What do we read in John 3:17 and Luke 9:56? What are the divine attributes given to us in Psalms 86:5 and 15?

SOUL WINNERS WILL BE REWARDED ETERNALLY ... Will you be one of them? OR, are you wasting your brief life in this world on something else other than obeying Christ's Great Commission?

"And they that be wise shall shine as the brightness of the firmament; and they that turn many to righteousness as the stars for ever and ever." Daniel 12:3

Ministering to Mark

DRUNKEN and Laid Out on the Street Corner ... That's how we found Mark, but thank God that's not how this young man was left!

DALLAS, TEXAS: Please lift Mark in prayer. Brother Chad and I were blessed to help Mark (pictured) after we found him lying out on a street corner. He had thrown up and was completely incapacitated. While Chad stayed with Mark, I rushed over to a nearby restaurant and got 2 large ice waters. Within minutes after we sat him up and began "making" him drink that cold water, he began to come back to life. Mark had apparently had too much to drink at the hockey game he had attended. Chad and I were both thankful to be blessed to have met this young man. He is an extremely sincere, seeking soul and yet subject to the control of sin...but please pray for him to soon be saved. We are in regular communication with him and he is hungry to know Christ and even stated this very thing several times that night.

Mark and Chad

Neither Chad nor I said anything to Mark about the LORD in the beginning. We were simply responding to the immediate need of protecting him from being arrested for public intoxication, etc. The cops even came over to speak with me and I assured them that we had this situation taken care of. They didn't intervene and graciously allowed us to continue taking care of Mark.

There are many Marks in this world and God is going to use each of His children to minister His love to those searching souls!

God's Love is Shining Brightly Through His Beloved Body

The light of Jesus Christ is shining brightly through His beloved people in this final hour!

Mark asked us if we were Christians even before we mentioned it. Several times Mark said, "The most loving people in the world, the only people who help others out, are Christians." He had apparently been greatly impacted in the past by the love of God in His people, and he made it abundantly clear (verbally) that he was greatly blessed that brother Chad and I were helping him.

> **"By this shall all men know that ye are my disciples, if ye have love one to another."**
> **John 13:35**

We were blessed to spend about three to four hours with Mark and ministered God's Word at length to him as he eagerly devoured it in his heart and mind. I pulled up the King James Bible on my phone and began reading it to him, side by side. After about four verses into Psalms chapter 40, Mark took over and began reading it out loud. I sat silent and read along with him as he hungrily read those divinely inspired words out loud.

Nightfall

Another thing that confirmed God's hand in this divine encounter is that Mark told us point blank that God has been convicting and drawing him for a long, long time. Mark was given several of the Ten Commandments verbatim and admitted to having broken all of them. We prayed with Mark asking God to clear the way for him to repent and be born again.

The Author and Mark

Thank you for praying for Mark. I've since been in touch with him several times. Be assured that our LORD is drawing Mark just as He did in each of our own salvation stories!

Before we look at another current example of the LORD moving upon the hearts of sinners to be saved, please keep this following all-important biblical truth in mind.

Ultimate Evangelism Key

The explosive divine power to foundationally change and evangelize the world, as evidenced in the earliest followers of Christ, is the focus of the Gospel of Jesus as it pertains to Him using you mightily. This unique, divine enablement and ability is historically and perpetually the key to powerful and revolutionary evangelism brought to completion by the LORD Himself through the diligent obedience of His people (Mark 16:15-20). This essential component is that of the daily cross. Such a death guarantees the resurrection life, love, and power of God raising your life upward to bear much fruit for His glory (John 15:1-16).

Listen to Paul:

> **"Always bearing about in the body the dying of the Lord Jesus, that the life also of Jesus might be made manifest in our body. [11] For we which live are alway delivered unto death for Jesus' sake, that the life also of Jesus might be made manifest in our mortal flesh. [12] So then death worketh in us, but life in you." 2 Corinthians 4:10-12**

Nightfall

God's Word is ALWAYS fresh, present tense, all-powerful, relevant, revolutionary, right now, alive (living, active) and effective to His glory (Isaiah 40:8; 55:11; Hebrews 4:12; 1 Peter 1:23; Mark 13:31, etc.).

Jesus Came for and Cares for the Lost

There has never in the history of mankind been an hour when the lost souls of this fleeting world need to be reached with Christ's glorious Gospel more than there is today – today is the day of salvation (2 Corinthians 6:2). And, such requires only one entity in the earth to accomplish – Jesus' people! That has not and never will be accomplished haphazardly or accidentally. It is a divine mandate and must be deliberately carried out by His people. In giving us His Great Commission mandate, Jesus promised He'd be with us in this mission – to the end of the world – till He soon returns (Matthew 28:18-20; Mark 16:15-20; John 20:21-22). We call it Christ's Great Commission and it's ours to do, today. Jesus says not to wait but to go – participate (John 4:34-38).

Perhaps God is speaking to the hearts of a few business men who see HIS work going on. Perhaps the godly response to the work of Jesus going on is to say to the servants of the LORD, "Brother(s) you keep doing what you're doing! I'm getting behind it with both feet and fueling this – HIS – work! I know Jesus is coming soon and I am with Him and behind HIS work all the way! I will use His resources for His glory and will be found with my hand on the plow of HIS work!"

If your personal attitude and actions are, "Yeah you brothers and sisters keep doing God's work while I keep living my life to my own self-serving glory …

Nightfall

I will see you in Heaven" …. you are in utter need of repenting.

> **"Submit yourselves therefore to God. Resist the devil, and he will flee from you. [8] Draw nigh to God, and he will draw nigh to you. Cleanse your hands, ye sinners; and purify your hearts, ye double minded. [9] Be afflicted, and mourn, and weep: let your laughter be turned to mourning, and your joy to heaviness. [10] Humble yourselves in the sight of the Lord, and he shall lift you up."**
> **James 4:7-10**

This is No Game!

Jesus is coming saints! This is not a game and this is not our home. We are here on mission – His Great Commission mandate! We will not get a redo. Do not allow some wolf plant posing as a representative of Christ to rob you.

> **"Behold, I come quickly: hold that fast which thou hast, that no man take thy crown." Revelation 3:11**

Never mind the self-serving notion toward Christ's workers of, "Yeah leave your post and go get a secular job too! Do both. I don't care if people get saved, sanctified, equipped, and taught God's Word, I just don't want MY money inconvenienced!"

Wow!

May the LORD rebuke and strike this evil thought down in Jesus' name and renew our minds to mature, to grow up into Christ and take personal responsibility to do our part in HIS kingdom work!

If you want to know if you are of God, ask yourself what HIS work means to you. There you will find if you know and love Him truly. ALL who know Him are possessed with His heart to reach the lost and grow up His saints. This is without exception.

These lost souls for whom Christ came and died matter to Him – and without exception they matter to those who truly know Him (Luke 19:10; 1 Timothy 1:15). Those who know and follow Christ are fishing for souls (Matthew 4:19).

What happens when someone follows Christ? What did Jesus say they are becoming?

> **"And he saith unto them, Follow me, and I will make you fishers of men." Matthew 4:19**

Nightfall

When we truly get right with God, lost souls for whom He came and bled and was raised again matter to us!

Salt and Light

May God refresh and inspire your life as you listen to the Son of God who saved you for His own special purpose.

> **"Ye are the salt of the earth: but if the salt have lost his savour, wherewith shall it be salted? it is thenceforth good for nothing, but to be cast out, and to be trodden under foot of men. [14] Ye are the light of the world. A city that is set on an hill cannot be hid. [15] Neither do men light a candle, and put it under a bushel, but on a candlestick; and it giveth light unto all that are in the house. [16] Let your light so shine before men, that they may see your good works, and glorify your Father which is in heaven." Matthew 5:13-16**

See *Revolutionary Evangelism* (insightful and encouraging book) to turbo charge your personal evangelism! This book can be obtained on SafeGuardYourSoul.com and Amazon.com.

God is so good, saints, and all we need to do is be prepared, prayerful, and available! Thank God for those who choose to support His work in this late hour before Christ's soon return. Feel free to access the "Because You Care" page at SafeGuardYourSoul.com (see button at top).

Nightfall

Prayer: *Holy Father, thank You for the unspeakable precious gift of Your only begotten Son given for my sins and salvation! Thank You kindly for continuing the good work You began in me the day You found and saved me for Your eternal purpose. In the name of Jesus Christ, I ask you to anoint my life to be dead and buried with Christ so that He alone reigns supreme. Please use me for Your eternal glory, Father. You must increase, LORD Jesus, but I must decrease! In Jesus' name, amen.*

CAPTURE POINTS

- Why did Jesus come to the earth? Luke 19:10 and 1 Timothy 1:15.

- What did Jesus tell us would be the result if we truly follow Him? Matthew 4:19 Discuss.

- Concerning our personal evangelism, what is the generator of divine power that will propel the life of Christ through our lives? 2 Corinthians 4:10-12

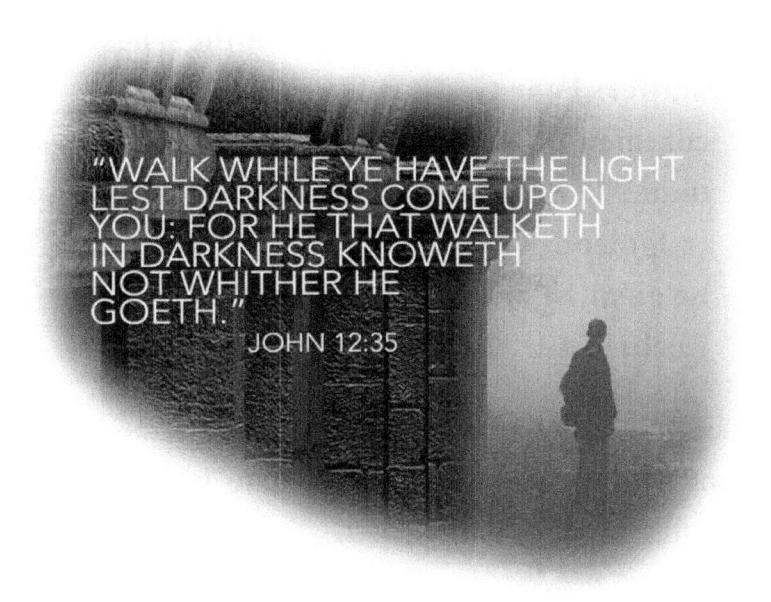

"WALK WHILE YE HAVE THE LIGHT LEST DARKNESS COME UPON YOU: FOR HE THAT WALKETH IN DARKNESS KNOWETH NOT WHITHER HE GOETH."
JOHN 12:35

Chapter 6

ଔ

Ready or Not –
Jesus is Coming!

> **"Let us hear the conclusion of the whole matter: Fear God, and keep his commandments: for this is the whole duty of man. [14] For God shall bring every work into judgment, with every secret thing, whether it be good, or whether it be evil."**
> **Ecclesiastes 12:13-14**

One thing is for certain and that's that Jesus is coming – and He's coming to judge and to make war and to shed the blood of the wicked.

1 Corinthians 15

> **"For as in Adam all die, even so in Christ shall all be made alive. [23] But every man in his own order: Christ the firstfruits; afterward they that are Christ's at his coming. [24] Then cometh the end, when he shall have delivered up the kingdom to God, even the Father; when he shall have put down all rule and all authority and power. [25] For he must reign, till he hath put all enemies under his feet. [26] The last enemy that shall be destroyed is death. [27] For he hath put all things under his feet. But when he saith all things are put under him, it is manifest that he is excepted, which did put**

all things under him. ²⁸ And when all things shall be subdued unto him, then shall the Son also himself be subject unto him that put all things under him, that God may be all in all." 1 Corinthians 15:22-28

The Return

God alone knows the day and the hour of Christ's return and yet we do know of a certainty that there *will* be a catching away. There will be a great separation between the righteous and the wicked (Matthew 13).

> "For the Lord himself shall descend from heaven with a shout, with the voice of the archangel, and with the trump of God: and the dead in Christ shall rise first: ¹⁷ Then we which are alive and remain shall be caught up together with them in the clouds, to meet the Lord in the air: and so shall we ever be with the Lord. ¹⁸ Wherefore comfort one another with these words."
> 1 Thessalonians 4:16-18

"**Comfort**" in this fleeting life, especially in these increasingly dark days, comes from knowing Christ and knowing that He is going to return soon for His own. Here in the passage above, His disciples are instructed to **"comfort one another with these words"** of the assurance of His soon return.

Preparing to Meet Our Maker

For whom is Jesus going to return? Have you ever asked that question in your mind?

The Son of God came to the earth to complete His Father's mission to redeem mankind. He was completely successful. While hanging on the cross for our sins, Jesus said, **"It is finished"** which means simply – the price for all of man's sin is now paid in full! (John 19:30)

Jesus was then buried and raised from the dead three days later. He now sits at the right hand of our heavenly Father in Heaven.

Hebrews 9

> **"For Christ is not entered into the holy places made with hands, which are the figures of the true; but into heaven itself, now to appear in the presence of God for us:** [25] **Nor yet that he should offer himself often, as the high priest entereth into the holy place every year with blood of others;** [26] **For then must he often have suffered since the**

> **foundation of the world: but now once in the end of the world hath he appeared to put away sin by the sacrifice of himself. ²⁷ And as it is appointed unto men once to die, but after this the judgment: ²⁸ So Christ was once offered to bear the sins of many; and unto them that look for him shall he appear the second time without sin unto salvation."**
> **Hebrews 9:24-28**

As we just read, Jesus is coming back for **"them that look for him."** Those that look for Him to return are those who are preparing to meet the Bridegroom and so they are preparing their lives for such an unsurpassed, significant event. This all begins with an honest assessment of our lives before Him – in the mirror of His Word.

Guilty as Charged

The LORD told us that He looks on the heart of man. Are our hearts basically good as some teach?

> **"The heart is deceitful above all things, and desperately wicked: who can know it?"**
> **Jeremiah 17:9**

Nightfall

The LORD declares us all guilty in His holy eyes and, therefore, worthy of punishment in the severity of the domain of the unrepentant damned (Hell).

> **"Now we know that what things soever the law saith, it saith to them who are under the law: that every mouth may be stopped, and all the world may become guilty before God." Romans 3:19**

With not one exception, all of mankind has sinned and the darkest days of depravity lie just ahead and are now escalating into the culmination of the darkest days of human History which are upon us. Mankind is going to self-destruct. He cannot save himself. He cannot solve his own problems which are rooted in his sin – which only the One whom we've sinned against can solve.

Romans 3

> **"For all have sinned, and come short of the glory of God; [24] Being justified freely by his grace through the redemption that is in Christ Jesus: [25] Whom God hath set forth to be a propitiation through faith in his blood, to declare his righteousness for the remission of sins that are past, through the forbearance of God; [26] To declare, I say, at**

> this time his righteousness: that he might be just, and the justifier of him which believeth in Jesus. ²⁷ Where is boasting then? It is excluded. By what law? of works? Nay: but by the law of faith. ²⁸ Therefore we conclude that a man is justified by faith without the deeds of the law." Romans 3:23-28

No one is good – not even one of us. We have all sinned against our Maker who is the Judge of our eternal souls. We are full of iniquity – with a bent and tendency toward rebellion and sin, a dilemma that God alone can solve.

Romans 3

> "As it is written, There is none righteous, no, not one: ¹¹ There is none that understandeth, there is none that seeketh after God. ¹² They are all gone out of the way, they are together become unprofitable; there is none that doeth good, no, not one. ¹³ Their throat is an open sepulchre; with their tongues they have used deceit; the poison of asps is under their lips: ¹⁴ Whose mouth is full of cursing and bitterness: ¹⁵ Their feet are swift to shed blood: ¹⁶ Destruction and misery are in their ways: ¹⁷ And the way of peace have they not

known: [18] There is no fear of God before their eyes. [19] Now we know that what things soever the law saith, it saith to them who are under the law: that every mouth may be stopped, and all the world may become guilty before God. [20] Therefore by the deeds of the law there shall no flesh be justified in his sight: for by the law is the knowledge of sin. [21] But now the righteousness of God without the law is manifested, being witnessed by the law and the prophets; [22] Even the righteousness of God which is by faith of Jesus Christ unto all and upon all them that believe: for there is no difference: [23] For all have sinned, and come short of the glory of God." Romans 3:10-23

God Sees All Wickedness and Will Judge It

"And GOD saw that the wickedness of man was great in the earth, and that every imagination of the thoughts of his heart was only evil continually. ... [12] And God looked upon the earth, and, behold, it was corrupt; for all flesh had corrupted his way upon the earth." Genesis 6:5, 12

This was the divine assessment of mankind after his fall in the Garden and before the flood judgment upon the unrepentant.

> **"Fear them not therefore: for there is nothing covered, that shall not be revealed; and hid, that shall not be known."**
> **Matthew 10:26**

Ultimately the Bible has only One Author and so the message from Genesis to Revelation is intertwined and synthesizes perfectly (Exodus 20:22; 2 Timothy 3:16; 2 Peter 1:20-21).

When speaking of these final days, the LORD Jesus Christ brings in the story of mankind after the fall of Adam and before He flooded the earth and allowed only eight souls to escape that divine judgment. Check this out:

Matthew 24

> **"Verily I say unto you, This generation shall not pass, till all these things be fulfilled.**
> **35 Heaven and earth shall pass away, but my words shall not pass away. 36 But of that day and hour knoweth no man, no, not the angels of heaven, but my Father only. 37 But as the**

days of Noe were, so shall also the coming of the Son of man be. ³⁸ For as in the days that were before the flood they were eating and drinking, marrying and giving in marriage, until the day that Noe entered into the ark, ³⁹ And knew not until the flood came, and took them all away; so shall also the coming of the Son of man be." Matthew 24:34-39

As the flood of water swept away and drowned millions of sinful souls in Noah's day, so shall the divine judgment shortly to come rout away most into the incarceration of the prison and lake of fire. God is going to dredge up the body of every lost soul, unite the two, and present them before the Supreme Court of His Universe. This is going to be the most fearful event in human history as His translucent light pierces the very core of every single sinner who had rejected the salvation He provided with the very blood of His only begotten Son. Every thought, motive, intent, and action of their lives will be brought to the light – openly displayed for all to see.

The Great White Throne Judgment

"And the devil that deceived them was cast into the lake of fire and brimstone, where the beast and the false prophet are, and shall be tormented day and night for ever and ever. [11] And I saw a great white throne, and him that sat on it, from whose face the earth and the heaven fled away; and there was found no place for them. [12] And I saw the dead, small and great, stand before God; and the books were opened: and another book was opened, which is the book of life: and the dead were judged out of those things which were written in the books, according to their works. [13] And the sea gave up the dead which were in it; and death and hell delivered up the dead which were in them: and they were judged every man according to their works. [14] And death and hell were cast into the lake of fire. This is the second death. [15] And whosoever was not found written in the book of life was cast into the lake of fire." Revelation 20:10-15

Sinful Scoffers

We are forewarned that some will scoff at the truth to their own eternal destruction while a few will scamper to the safety of the only Savior.

Nightfall

2 Peter 3

"This second epistle, beloved, I now write unto you; in both which I stir up your pure minds by way of remembrance: [2] That ye may be mindful of the words which were spoken before by the holy prophets, and of the commandment of us the apostles of the Lord and Saviour: [3] Knowing this first, that there shall come in the last days scoffers, walking after their own lusts, [4] And saying, Where is the promise of his coming? for since the fathers fell asleep, all things continue as they were from the beginning of the creation. [5] For this they willingly are ignorant of, that by the word of God the heavens were of old, and the earth standing out of the water and in the water: [6] Whereby the world that then was, being overflowed with water, perished: [7] But the heavens and the earth, which are now, by the same word are kept in store, reserved unto fire against the day of judgment and perdition of ungodly men. [8] But, beloved, be not ignorant of this one thing, that one day is with the Lord as a thousand years, and a thousand years as one day. [9] The Lord is not slack concerning his promise, as some men count slackness; but is longsuffering to us-ward, not willing that any should perish, but that all should come to repentance. ¹⁰ But the day of the Lord will come as a thief in the night; in the which the heavens shall pass away with a great noise, and the elements shall melt with fervent heat, the earth also and the works that are therein shall be burned up. ¹¹ Seeing then that all these things shall be dissolved, what manner of persons ought ye to be in all holy conversation and godliness, ¹² Looking for and hasting unto the coming of the day of God, wherein the heavens being on fire shall be dissolved, and the elements shall melt with fervent heat? ¹³ Nevertheless we, according to his promise, look for new heavens and a new earth, wherein dwelleth righteousness. ¹⁴ Wherefore, beloved, seeing that ye look for such things, be diligent that ye may be found of him in peace, without spot, and blameless. ¹⁵ And account that the longsuffering of our Lord is salvation; even as our beloved brother Paul also according to the wisdom given unto him hath written unto you; ¹⁶ As also in all his epistles, speaking in them of these things; in which

are some things hard to be understood, which they that are unlearned and unstable wrest, as they do also the other scriptures, unto their own destruction. [17] Ye therefore, beloved, seeing ye know these things before, beware lest ye also, being led away with the error of the wicked, fall from your own stedfastness. [18] But grow in grace, and in the knowledge of our Lord and Saviour Jesus Christ. To him be glory both now and for ever. Amen." 2 Peter 3:1-18

Don't Dip Your Toe in the Water – Just Jump all the Way in at Once!

The Gospel – following Christ – is nothing to be casual about. It's not something you can just try out. You must turn your whole being over to the One who made you and will judge you for the life you chose to live in this sinful, fleeting world. You will give full account to Him.

To escape the coming judgment of the Almighty, one must repent, receive Christ and abide in a saving relationship with Him to the end of his earthly life.

Mark 8

> "For whosoever will save his life shall lose it; but whosoever shall lose his life for my sake and the gospel's, the same shall save it. [36] For what shall it profit a man, if he shall gain the whole world, and lose his own soul? [37] Or what shall a man give in exchange for his soul? [38] Whosoever therefore shall be ashamed of me and of my words in this adulterous and sinful generation; of him also shall the Son of man be ashamed, when he cometh in the glory of his Father with the holy angels." Mark 8:35-38

Christianity, as defined by God in His Word, is a life lived, a lifestyle, a life-long experience and relationship, not a religion or one-time event. That life and walk begins at the moment of true repentance which is an unreserved, wholesale surrendering of one's life to the LORD who alone is worthy.

> "Testifying both to the Jews, and also to the Greeks, repentance toward God, and faith toward our Lord Jesus Christ." Acts 20:21

> "And brought them out, and said, Sirs, what must I do to be saved? [31] And they said,

Nightfall

Believe on the Lord Jesus Christ, and thou shalt be saved, and thy house." Acts 16:30-31

"I tell you, Nay: but, except ye repent, ye shall all likewise perish." Luke 13:3

"For by grace are ye saved through faith; and that not of yourselves: it is the gift of God: [9] Not of works, lest any man should boast. [10] For we are his workmanship, created in Christ Jesus unto good works, which God hath before ordained that we should walk in them." Ephesians 2:8-10

Nothing short of a genuine born-again experience and subsequent daily walk of denying oneself and taking up the cross to follow Jesus is going to qualify for participating in a relationship with Christ and thereby being preserved to the end and gloriously ushered into His New Jerusalem. One cannot truly follow Christ any other way except that way which He plainly prescribed and yet is rarely heard in the modern church world. Church membership and the weekly attendance of it has taken the place of that daily cross walk (Luke 9:23-24).

Prayer: *Father in Heaven, I am completely guilty of sinning against You. I beg You now, this very instant, to be merciful to me, a sinner. I have lied, used Your holy name in vain, sworn, cursed, hated, not forgiven others, coveted what was not mine, had other false gods before You, and committed adultery in my heart by lusting, etc. I admit to my total and complete guilt before Your holy eyes and right this moment, turn my life over to You without reservation. Into Your holy hands I submit my spirit, soul, and body to You. I am all Yours now LORD Jesus. My life is no longer mine, but Yours. At this very instant, I abandon my own will for Yours. You must increase but I must decrease. I am dead and my life is hid with Christ in God. I am crucified with Christ and nevertheless I live and yet not I but Christ liveth in me. The life I here forward live in the flesh, I live by the faith of the very Son of God. In Jesus Christ's blessed name we pray. Amen!*

CAPTURE POINTS

- What does the Bible teach about the fallen nature of mankind? Genesis 6:5, 12; Jeremiah 17:9; Romans 3
- Does the Bible prophetically speak of scoffers in end time? If so, what are we told they will be saying? 2 Peter 3

Nightfall

- How is a lost sinner saved into the kingdom of Christ? Ephesians 2:8-9
- What must the true believer do to abide or to remain in close relationship with Jesus Christ? John 15:1-6

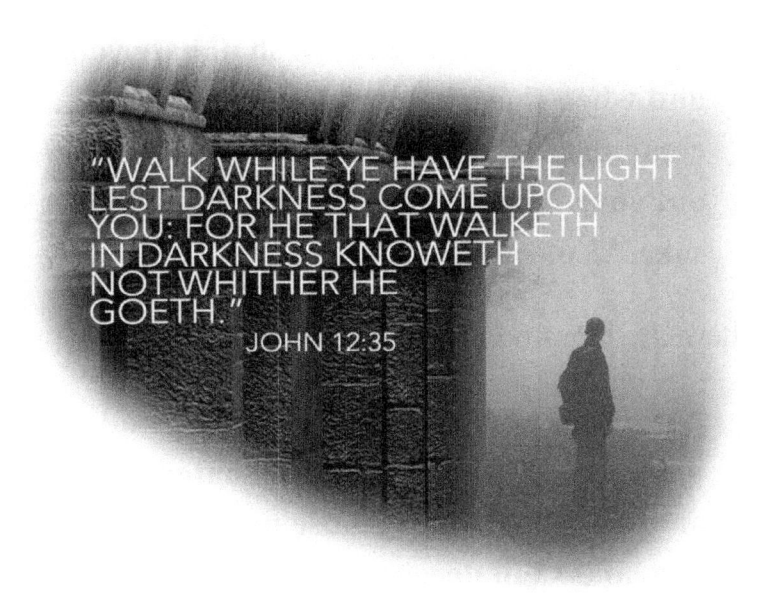

> "WALK WHILE YE HAVE THE LIGHT LEST DARKNESS COME UPON YOU: FOR HE THAT WALKETH IN DARKNESS KNOWETH NOT WHITHER HE GOETH."
> JOHN 12:35

Chapter 7

Get Ready for Warfare

Nightfall

"Blessed are ye, when men shall hate you, and when they shall separate you from their company, and shall reproach you, and cast out your name as evil, for the Son of man's sake." Luke 6:22

There are blessings in the persecutions.

"And then shall many be offended, and shall betray one another, and shall hate one another. [11] And many false prophets shall rise, and shall deceive many. [12] And because iniquity shall abound, the love of many shall wax cold. [13] But he that shall endure unto the end, the same shall be saved." Matthew 24:10-13

WHEN YOU SEE a true brother or sister in Christ being persecuted, maligned, and slandered by Satan's agents in our midst, 1) covet to be more rooted in Christ and therefore bearing **"much fruit"** as they are (John 15:1-16), and, 2) celebrate with them the reality that God is using them in a great way and that's why they are being attacked by the accuser of the brethren (Matthew 5:10-12; Acts 5:41; Revelation 12:10-12).

Jesus is Coming!

> "Beloved, think it not strange concerning the fiery trial which is to try you, as though some strange thing happened unto you: [13] But rejoice, inasmuch as ye are partakers of Christ's sufferings; that, when his glory shall be revealed, ye may be glad also with exceeding joy. [14] If ye be reproached for the name of Christ, happy are ye; for the spirit of glory and of God resteth upon you: on their part he is evil spoken of, but on your part he is glorified." 1 Peter 4:12-14

ACCORDING TO THE TEACHINGS OF JESUS AND HIS HOLY APOSTLES, if we are not being persecuted, we should WORRY and examine ourselves. And if we are being persecuted, we should REJOICE! Luke 6:26, etc.

As foretold by our LORD Jesus, there are so many cold, dark people in this fleeting world in this late hour, and it's going to get worse. When I see someone who receives hate from many, it makes me wonder if that persecuted person is speaking an unpopular truth. So, I investigate (Matthew 24:10-13; 2 Timothy 3:13). Jesus promised that when you are loved by the masses, that may be a strong indication that you have fallen prey to

Nightfall

the trap of tickling ears instead of obeying God by simply preaching His pure Word (2 Timothy 4:2-4). Those who live out and preach the pure divine truth of God's written Word will be lied about and ostracized and hated (Luke 6:21-26).

"Truth is hate speech to those who hate truth." Author unknown

Have you noticed that rebellious people hate when truth seekers are SPECIFIC about GOD's judgment coming on their wickedness? Why? – **"And this is the condemnation, that light is come into the world, and men loved darkness rather than light, because their deeds were evil. [20] For every one that doeth evil hateth the light, neither cometh to the light, lest his deeds should be reproved. [21] But he that doeth truth cometh to the light, that his deeds may be made manifest, that they are wrought in God."** (John 3:19-21)

Just what do we know about the apostle Paul's life?

> **"But thou hast fully known my doctrine, manner of life, purpose, faith, longsuffering, charity, patience, [11] Persecutions, afflictions, which came unto me at Antioch, at Iconium, at Lystra; what persecutions I endured: but**

> **out of them all the Lord delivered me. ¹² Yea, and ALL that will live godly in Christ Jesus shall suffer persecution. ¹³ But evil men and seducers shall wax worse and worse, deceiving, and being deceived."**
> **2 Timothy 3:10-13**

Did you note here in this passage that for preaching pure **"doctrine"** the apostle Paul was assailed constantly? Such will be the case in this fleeting life for all who truly serve Jesus Christ. It's a Bible promise Christ-rejecting deceivers like Joel Osteen, emergent devils, and word of faith beguilers will never mention. You will never see such a Bible promise on the refrigerator of a gullible dupe who follows modern wolves. They love their lives in this world and will therefore be cast into the lake of fire to suffer conscious torment forever (John 12:23-25; Revelation 12:11).

On this topic of serving Christ and being consequently persecuted, one sister in Christ writes:

"All who live godly in Christ Jesus shall suffer persecution. This we have as a mark, if you will. If you want to find true Christians you will find the persecuted bunch, tried in the fire. I believe Jesus is the greatest example of a persecuted Christian. He was

Nightfall

hated and if you are in Him, you will be hated too. The ones who really are doing a work for God, will be attacked by every demonic power to stop them. After all, why would Satan want to give ease to a true, born-again, Spirit-filled (filled with the Baptism of His Holy Spirit) and on fire Christian? Some of us aren't sitting in our easy chairs, some of us are in the fire, so come on in and join the persecuted too and you just might be one of the blessed who are killed by the many who will think they are doing God's service."

"It is a faithful saying: For if we be dead with him, we shall also live with him: [12] **If we suffer, we shall also reign with him: if we deny him, he also will deny us."**
2 Timothy 2:11-12

If we suffer now, we will rejoice later and for all eternity! We should embrace Christ's promise that because we serve Him, we will suffer persecution. We have been told by the LORD to realize that rather than to be reigning now (*Best Life Now* LIE) and suffering eternally (excruciating torment), we are called to suffer with Jesus now and reign later and forever. He left that choice to each of us. Only you can choose for you (Deuteronomy 30:19; Joshua 24:15).

Are You on Satan's Hit List?

GET READY FOR SPIRITUAL WARFARE – that is, if you are obeying God by communicating His truth. Get in the fight saint! The LORD will stand with you no matter what (Acts 7:54-60; 2 Timothy 4:16-18). Spiritual warfare many times comes in the form of confusion and through **"false brethren"** who think they are saved and yet are not. Many times, the evil one uses professed Christians to attack those few who are truly on the narrow road that leads to eternal life (Matthew 7:13-14). You will need to know how to rightly divide the Word of truth which comes from studying to show ourselves approved unto God, being taught of Him (2 Timothy 2:15).

For example, when you preach the Word, showing how GOD (not you or mere man) but GOD Himself clearly told us that certain classes of sinners will be in Hell, you will be opposed. One thing some will attempt to do is tell you to stop trying to divide the wheat and the tares as Jesus says the angels will do that (Matthew 13). Yet, think about this: Preaching the judgment or Word of God is not the same as attempting to divide the wheat from the tares (Matthew 13). Preaching the truth that God will damn those who die in sin is what God calls you and me to do. He will use His angels to divide the righteous from the wicked in the end but that doesn't mean He contradicted Himself nor does it negate our responsibility to speak His holy truth.

When the heat of the truth comes, unrepentant, obstinate people living in sin will get outraged. When the light of truth hits that darkness, some folk get livid and begin to attack the messenger. Why? Let's read it again. Jesus says:

> **"And this is the condemnation, that light is come into the world, and men loved darkness rather than light, because their (own) deeds were evil. [20] For every one that doeth evil hateth the light, neither cometh to the light, lest his deeds should be reproved. [21] But he that doeth truth cometh to the light, that his deeds may be made manifest, that they are wrought in God." John 3:19-21**

When men love darkness more than the light of Christ's truth, even though they claim to be saved, they will many times react violently to the truth, seeking to defend darkness by twisting and misusing Scripture.

Anybody know what I am talking about here? Have you seen this pattern?

The Bible commands us to **"Preach the word ... in season and out of season."** (2 Timothy 4:1-4) Then, when we do, Satan raises up people to come against that Word of truth and try to confuse the issue as he and his human pawns oppose the truth while claiming to be defending it. Preaching the Gospel and calling out those who claim to be Christians and yet are living in open sin, is the exact thing Jesus did when addressing the Pharisees who feigned to be representing the LORD while brazenly teaching and living contrary to what the LORD Himself told them in His Word. Read in Matthew 23 where Jesus lambasts the Jewish **"hypocrites"** and told them three times that they were going to Hell. Then, in contrast, Jesus deals very differently with the sinners who have never come to Him yet and do not claim to be representing Him (John 4: 8, etc.).

When attacked, and called judgmental, I have learned to boldly declare: "I am not the judge but God is the Judge and I am preaching HIS judgment for which we are ALL accountable!"

Preaching the Word of God is preaching the judgment of God. Speak with His words to others and fret not for those who persecute you (Isaiah 51:7, 12).

Nightfall

> "Hearken unto me, ye that know righteousness, the people in whose heart is my law; fear ye not the reproach of men, neither be ye afraid of their revilings." Isaiah 51:7

> "I, even I, am he that comforteth you: who art thou, that thou shouldest be afraid of a man that shall die, and of the son of man which shall be made as grass; [13] And forgettest the LORD thy maker, that hath stretched forth the heavens, and laid the foundations of the earth; and hast feared continually every day because of the fury of the oppressor, as if he were ready to destroy? and where is the fury of the oppressor?" Isaiah 51:12-13

The truth divides between the mere professors and the genuine possessors of salvation. Read Christ's words carefully:

> "He that is of God heareth God's words: ye therefore hear them not, because ye are not of God." John 8:47

According to the above statement, who did Jesus tell us is "of God" and who did He show us is **"not of God"**?

"Think not that I am come to send peace on earth: I came not to send peace, but a sword." Matthew 10:34

The **"sword"** here represents judgment and division. The truth – via those who believe it and those who don't – separates those two classes of people. Embracing or rejecting Bible truth shows us the fruit of our own lives and the lives of others, revealing to the true saint who is truly **"of God"** and who is **"NOT of God"** and what Paul called **"false brethren."** (John 8:47; 2 Corinthians 11:26; Galatians 2:4)

"If you don't know or follow the Bible, anything goes." Pastor Joseph Gros

What passes as "Christian" and is accepted these days among some people simply shows the hearts of the people and how they have only a mere "form of godliness" but do not know His holy reign in their personal lives (2 Timothy 3:1-7; 4:3). This means they have not truly repented, which means coming to full surrender, turning from their own way and wholly to Him and His ways. If they knew Him, they would not be blinded and following falsehoods that contradict His Word (2 Thessalonians 2:10-12).

Nightfall

"And with all deceivableness of unrighteousness in them that perish; because they received not the love of the truth, that they might be saved. [11] And for this cause God shall send them strong delusion, that they should believe a lie: [12] That they all might be damned who believed not the truth, but had pleasure in unrighteousness."
2 Thessalonians 2:10-12

Prayer: *Father, in Jesus' holy name, please bless Your people to grow in Thy grace, to be more deeply rooted in the love of Christ, and to be blessed to endure the delusions and afflictions that come as we serve You! May grace upon grace be multiplied to Your servants the world over in this last hour before the return of our KING! In Jesus' name I pray.*

CAPTURE POINTS

- How did Jesus say we will know we are "blessed"? Read Luke 6:22 and discuss/meditate upon.

- In 1 Peter 4:12-14, why are born-again believers told to "Rejoice"?

- Concerning spiritual warfare, decipher and discuss the contrasting reactions of those who hear the word and receive the light of divine truth. Read the words of Christ recorded in John 3:19-21.

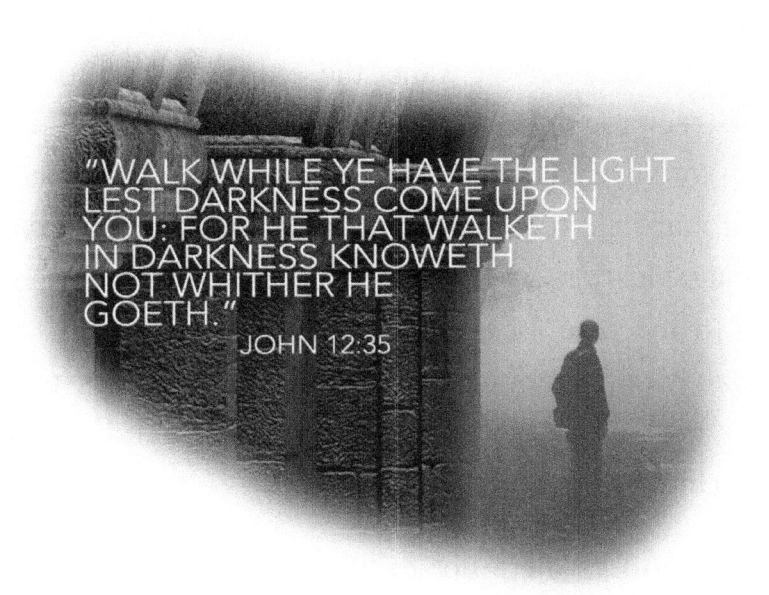

> "WALK WHILE YE HAVE THE LIGHT LEST DARKNESS COME UPON YOU: FOR HE THAT WALKETH IN DARKNESS KNOWETH NOT WHITHER HE GOETH."
>
> JOHN 12:35

Chapter 8

ঔ

Mary Moments in a Martha World

Don't Bother Obeying If You Don't Love Him!

Nightfall

Being human, when one is in love with someone, naturally, that person wants the one they love to love them reciprocally. When you are in love, you want them to want you. That's what makes chemistry and a good marriage relationship – a man and a woman who spontaneously reciprocate love to each other – because they truly love one another. Think about that. No human would deny such a simple, self-evident truth. Well, the One who made us wants us to want Him – to love Him.

Just WHAT is there not to love about the LORD and Savior Jesus Christ? If we haven't taken time to get to know about Him and to know Him, we will never begin to uncover His infinite riches, truth, divine attributes, kindness, mercy, grace, love, and much more.

Jesus says: **"IF YOU LOVE ME, keep my commandments."** (John 14:15) The self-reliant legalist is quick to emphasize the keeping of His commands, but doing so is utterly in vain if we have not love for Him! Read Jesus' words again and look closely at what comes first which indicates divine priority – **"IF YOU LOVE ME, keep my commandments."** (John 14:15) You see, it's only **"IF"** we **"LOVE"** Him that He is interested in our obedience. Obedience to what Christ commanded is of no value to God if we don't sincerely love Him.

Perhaps our prayer should begin with *"Father, You are love. Help me to love You more! Jesus, You must increase but I must decrease! I beg You now to break me, LORD!"*

EVERY single human being loves someone supremely. For most who claim to know Jesus love self, more than the Savior (2 Timothy 3:1-7). Token obedience out of guilt doesn't please God.

When Jesus compared Mary and Martha, which one did He indicate pleased Him most?

> **"And Jesus answered and said unto her, Martha, Martha, thou art careful and troubled about many things: ⁴² But <u>one thing is needful: and Mary hath chosen that good part, which shall not be taken away from her</u>." Luke 10:41-42**

Note that Jesus here said that the **"good part"** Mary chose **"shall not be taken away from her."** Now, recall with me how Paul taught that love is eternal whereas gifts are not (1 Corinthians 13).

Heartfelt Willingness Must Precede Obedience

You know, when His people were backslidden, the LORD told them to **"Come ... If ye be willing and obedient, ye shall eat the good of the land."** (Isaiah 1:18-20) Note the order here: Of first and foremost importance to God is that His people be **"willing."** Note the order and how **"willing"** comes before **"obedient."** God is only interested in our obedience if and as our hearts are **"willing"** or desiring Him.

1. **"willing"**

2. **"obedient"**

"Your Work of Faith, and Labour of Love"

> **"Remembering without ceasing <u>your work of faith, and labour of love</u>, and patience of hope in our Lord Jesus Christ, in the sight of God and our Father;" 1 Thessalonians 1:3**

Our work for Christ must emanate from our **"faith"** in Him and our **"love"** will bear the fruit of **"labour"** for His glory. You may wish to grab on to this divinely-inspired phrase – **"work of faith, and labour of love."**

The bottom line is that Jesus is not at all interested in you trying to serve and please Him IF YOU DON'T LOVE HIM. Of course, you must repent to be His son/daughter to begin with (Luke 13:3, 5). And repentance is putting your full trust in Him and the beginning of loving Him. The LORD looks upon and wants your heart. – **"Rend your heart, and not your garments."** (Joel 2:13)

I believe we can behold this important priority throughout our LORD's Word and Joel 2 is not an exception.

Read Luke 10:38-42

> **"Therefore also now, saith the Lord, turn ye even to me with all your heart, and with fasting, and with weeping, and with mourning: ¹³ And <u>rend your heart (internal), and not your garments (external things)</u>, and turn unto the Lord your God: for he is gracious and merciful, slow to anger, and of great kindness, and repenteth him of the evil. ¹⁴ Who knoweth if he will return and repent, and leave a blessing behind him; even a meat offering and a drink offering unto the Lord your God? ¹⁵ Blow the trumpet in Zion, sanctify a fast, call a solemn**

Nightfall

> assembly: ¹⁶ Gather the people, sanctify the congregation, assemble the elders, gather the children, and those that suck the breasts: let the bridegroom go forth of his chamber, and the bride out of her closet." **Joel 2:12-16**

In Matthew 9:13 Jesus told us to go and learn something:

> "But go ye and learn what that meaneth, <u>I will have mercy, and not sacrifice</u>: for I am not come to call the righteous, but sinners to repentance." **Matthew 9:13**

Christ foretold that in the last days, the love of many would wax cold – toward Him and consequently, His beloved people.

> "And then shall many be offended, and shall betray one another, and shall hate one another. ¹¹ And many false prophets shall rise, and shall deceive many. ¹² And <u>because iniquity shall abound, the love of many shall wax cold</u>. ¹³ But he that shall endure unto the end (truly loving Him supremely), the same shall be saved." **Matthew 24:10-13**

Jesus here says that the love for God among those who once knew Him is fading and waxing cold whereas it was once hot. Is this not exactly what happened to the Ephesians and the Laodiceans? (Revelation 2:4-5; 3:15-16). It's those who are choosing daily to love God above themselves who are longing to be with their glorious Savior. Their love for the LORD waxes hotter daily as they look expectantly and eagerly for His soon return.

Commanded to Love

IF we truly love Him, we *will* obey Him. Yet, trying to obey Him without loving Him in order to get Him to love us or please Him is futile.

Many are getting caught up in a law-keeping type of obedience. Many times we hear the term "keep Torah." BUT what did Jesus sum it all as? Many can be heard saying "Stop Sinning" and "Go and sin no more." Jesus said the latter but not before He forgave the woman He told that to. Redemption comes before obedience and overcoming (John 8:1-11; 1 John 5:4-5).

> **"Jesus said unto him, Thou shalt love the Lord thy God with all thy heart, and with all thy soul, and with all thy mind. [38] This is the first and great commandment. [39] And the**

second is like unto it, Thou shalt love thy neighbour as thyself. [40] <u>On these two commandments hang all the law and the prophets.</u>" Matthew 22:37-40

And just WHY are we privileged to return love to the LORD? – **"We love him, because <u>he first loved us</u>."** (1 John 4:19)

Study Luke 10:38-42.

"His Commandments are not Grievous"

Those who love the LORD desire and rejoice to obey Him. **"For this is the love of God, that we keep his commandments: and his commandments are not grievous."** (1 John 5:3) Now, go read this passage – begin reading in 1 John 5:1. Notice that it's only when we are not submitted to, that is, abiding intimately in, Christ that His commands would be **"grievous"** to us. Otherwise, our obedience to Him is a labor of love. Do you remember how much Jacob loved Rachel? That was his baby, wasn't it? Look what Scripture reveals about that relationship – **"And Jacob served seven years for Rachel; and they seemed unto him but a few days, for the love he had to her."** (Genesis 29:20)

Don't you just love that verse? – **"And Jacob served seven years for Rachel; and they seemed unto him but a few days, for the love he had to her."** (Genesis 29:20)

Rachel was a labor of love for Jacob. He didn't mind working for her because he loved her. Spending those years to be with Rachel was not **"grievous"** to Jacob because he loved Rachel.

"Anathema Maranatha"

Are you saying **"Come, Lord Jesus"** with those who truly love Him, or, are you cursed? (Revelation 22:20)

> **"If any man love not the Lord Jesus Christ, let him be Anathema Maranatha."**
> **1 Corinthians 16:22**

Of this verse, the late Donald Stamps notes:

"ANATHEMA. Paul ends the Corinthian letter by reminding all professing believers that to claim to be believers, yet to "love not the Lord,' is to be 'Anathema' (i.e., accursed, doomed). To 'love not the Lord' means to fail to have a heartfelt love toward Him, to not obey Him (John 14:21), and to distort the apostolic gospel of N.T. revelation. To be accursed means being excluded from the true spiritual church on

Nightfall

earth and finally from the heavenly kingdom of the age to come. Paul wants his readers to understand that the ultimate test of Christian discipleship is a personal, heartfelt loyalty to the Lord Jesus Christ (cf. Rom. 10:9)."

The last word in this verse is **"Maranatha"** which means "Come Lord." This is the heart cry of all who are His blessed remnant! Their hearts are looking for Him and they **"love his appearing."** (2 Timothy 4:8; Hebrews 9:28) Jesus will soon return for **"all them also that love his appearing."** (2 Timothy 4:8)

As things continue to get darker and the hearts of men more murderous and antichrist, we must rejoice and reflect upon the words of Jesus when He told us: **"And when these things begin to come to pass, then look up, and lift up your heads; for your redemption draweth nigh."** (Luke 21:28)

It is of the utmost importance that we choose to love and to continue to learn to love and obey our LORD Jesus Christ who bled to save us to the Father.

Friend, are you truly loving God first and foremost? Is Jesus truly first in your daily, personal life? Does the LORD come before YOU? Are you dying so He can live? Do you arise in the mornings to seek His holy face in prayer and reading His Word?

Nightfall

Prayer: *Heavenly Father, please bless the lives of all Your beloved saints to be still and know that You alone are God. Bless me to be settled at Your beautiful feet, anchored in an intimate, abiding fellowship with You as a foretaste of glory divine! I love You, Jesus, and thank You now and forevermore for Your amazing love and mercy You've had for Your people who are desperately dependent upon You in all things. In Jesus' name, amen.*

CAPTURE POINTS

- Read our LORD's words in John 14:15 and consider the correlation between love and obedience.

- When contrasting the worship of Mary and Martha, what does Jesus reveal about God's will? What most pleases Him? Read and discuss Luke 10:38-42.

- What is it that made a several-year period seem like just a brief time to Jacob? Read Genesis 29:20. How does this relate with Christ and His work of redemption of fallen mankind? Read Hebrews 12:1-3.

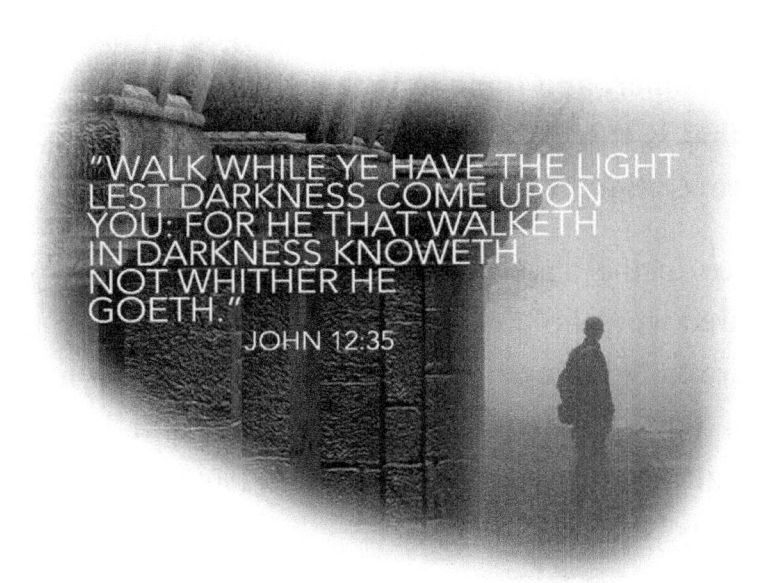

"WALK WHILE YE HAVE THE LIGHT LEST DARKNESS COME UPON YOU: FOR HE THAT WALKETH IN DARKNESS KNOWETH NOT WHITHER HE GOETH."
JOHN 12:35

Chapter 9

ଓଃ

Narrow is the Way

Nightfall

"Wherefore gird up the loins of your mind, be sober, and hope to the end for the grace that is to be brought unto you at the revelation of Jesus Christ." 1 Peter 1:13

Notice in the above instruction from the Holy Spirit inspired words to the saints from the apostle Peter, that we are to **"gird up"** or to cover and protect our minds **"and hope to the end for the grace that is to be brought unto you at the revelation (soon appearing) of Jesus Christ."**

God is in control saints. You can rest assured of that. Read Psalms 2! The LORD is laughing at the wicked and their plans to rule! They are infinitely outclassed and unqualified. They will look like they are prospering but oh how their day is coming and it's all over at that point. Jesus is coming but first, perilous times have to come (1 Timothy 4:1-3).

In this dark hour – the darkest, most depraved hour of human history – the wise virgin believers are clearly known by their hearkening ever closer to the breast and voice of their soon coming Bridegroom, Jesus Christ. They are being preserved by the LORD. These who freely follow Him, love Him and therefore they obey their Shepherd and no other will they follow (John 10:4-5; 14:15, 21; 1 John 2:3-6, etc.). Those who choose to be His sheep, follow Him ever nearer on that **"narrow"** way that leads to eternal life of which He told us **"few there be that find it."**

> **"Enter ye in at the strait gate: for wide is the gate, and broad is the way, that leadeth to destruction, and MANY there be which go in thereat:** [14] **Because strait is the gate, and narrow is the way, which leadeth unto life, and FEW there be that find it."**
> **Matthew 7:13-14**

Considering Christ's and His holy apostle's repeated, severe warnings to remain **"ready,"** it is utterly befuddling how so many leave people believing that they are unconditionally eternally secure and "as sure for Heaven as if they were already there." Those who lead people to believe they are unconditionally secure and ready to meet Christ no matter what spiritual state they are presently in, are clearly false teachers. To be a false teacher simply means that someone is teaching contrary to what Jesus and His apostles taught and thereby misleading the eternal souls of men against and away from Christ instead of gathering them to Him (Matthew 12:30). The LORD taught that false teachers scatter abroad instead of gather men to Christ (Matthew 12:30).

> "Wherefore gird up the loins of your mind, be sober, and hope to the end for the grace that is to be brought unto you at the revelation of Jesus Christ; [14] As obedient children, not fashioning yourselves according to the former lusts in your ignorance: [15] But as he which hath called you is holy, so be ye holy in all manner of conversation; [16] Because it is written, Be ye holy; for I am holy. [17] And if ye call on the Father, who without respect of persons judgeth according to every man's work, pass the time of your sojourning here in fear."
> 1 Peter 1:13-17

The wise virgin believer remains **"ready"** for the return of the Bridegroom at every momentary waking moment. She remains vigilant, prayerful, and ever watching for the soon return of her very **"first love."** (Revelation 2:4-5)

> "For where your treasure is, there will your heart be also. [35] Let your loins be girded about, and your lights burning; [36] And ye yourselves like unto men that wait for their lord, when he will return from the wedding; that when he cometh and knocketh, they

may open unto him immediately. ³⁷ Blessed are those servants, whom the lord when he cometh shall find watching: verily I say unto you, that he shall gird himself, and make them to sit down to meat, and will come forth and serve them. ³⁸ And if he shall come in the second watch, or come in the third watch, and find them so, blessed are those servants. ³⁹ And this know, that if the goodman of the house had known what hour the thief would come, he would have watched, and not have suffered his house to be broken through. ⁴⁰ Be ye therefore ready also: for the Son of man cometh at an hour when ye think not." Luke 12:34-40

This fellow follower of Jesus Christ would like to invite the reader to memorize these words of our LORD recorded in verse 40. Suggestion: write them with the reference on an index card to carry around and read, meditate upon, memorize, and to share with others.

Why such warnings if it were automatically assumed that all of those once saved by Christ were going to be ready when He returns? Why these warnings if there were no jeopardy of soul at hand and no possibility of losing out in the end? If all who were ever saved were automatically going to endure to the end, why such a warning to His own people concerning being shut out of His eternal kingdom?

Truth or Tradition?

Many insist upon bending Scripture to fit their false theology and tradition instead of trashing the tradition and embracing the truth.

> **"Beware lest any man spoil you through philosophy and vain deceit, after the tradition of men, after the rudiments of the world, and not after Christ." Colossians 2:8**
>
> **"Let God be true and every man a liar." Romans 3:4**

Jesus rebuked those who vainly thought they were right with God and yet following erroneous tradition they had been taught by mere men instead of divine truth given us by God.

Tradition leads to Hell. Obeying the truth ensures salvation and security with He who is **"the truth."** (John 14:6)

> "He answered and said unto them, Well hath Esaias prophesied of you hypocrites, as it is written, This people honoureth me with their lips, but their heart is far from me.
> 7 Howbeit in vain do they worship me, teaching for doctrines the commandments of men. 8 For laying aside the commandment of God, ye hold the tradition of men, as the washing of pots and cups: and many other such like things ye do. 9 And he said unto them, Full well ye reject the commandment of God, that ye may keep your own tradition." Mark 7:6-9

The counterfeit, actor, and imposter follows the tradition he's learned of mere sinful men posing as spiritual authority. He is willing to set aside the words of the very LORD He claims to be serving to follow tradition – teachings not found in God's Word.

> "Then said Jesus to those Jews which believed on him, If ye continue in my word, then are ye my disciples indeed; 32 And ye shall know the truth, and the truth shall make you free." John 8:31-32

Embracing and obeying divine truth makes one free and leads to eternal glory in Heaven with Christ who is

Nightfall

"the truth" and who gave us His written Word which **"is truth."** (John 8:31-32; 14:6; 17:17) His remnant is cleansed and sanctified by His truth.

> **"Now ye are clean through the word which I have spoken unto you." John 15:3**

> **"Sanctify them through thy truth: thy word is truth." John 17:17**

Biblically speaking, there is a clear delineation between those who truly know and presently follow Jesus Christ and those who don't. **"God is not the author of confusion."** (1 Corinthians 14:33)

Those who love God are known for their love for His Word. They hear His Word and forsake all that does not align. They follow Jesus Christ, their Shepherd and no other. The Son of God says this of those who choose to be His: **"The sheep follow him: for they know his voice. 5 And a stranger will they not follow, but will flee from him: for they know not the voice of strangers."** (John 10:4-5)

Here is the defining factor as put forth by the LORD Himself. Here's exactly what distinguishes between the authentic and the counterfeit. Please read these ensuing words of our Savior slowly and prayerfully:

"He that is of God heareth God's words: ye therefore hear them not, because ye are not of God." John 8:47

This is most certainly a memory verse for the elect of God.

Those who take God's Word seriously manifest clearly that they are choosing to fear, worship, and obey Him – the only One who can save them from sin and certain, everlasting damnation. They are His students – **"Come ... Learn of me"** says Christ (Matthew 11:28-30) The ears of the remnant of Christ are bent to Him. They live to please Him. They walk in His holy fear. They don't boast of their pastor or church or being a good church member, but boast only of the LORD Himself (1 Corinthians 1:29, 31). They are redeemed by His precious blood and refuse to give honor to another (1 Peter 1:18-19). He is their very first priority and love (Revelation 2:4-5). These who truly follow Jesus are listening to, and hearing His beautiful voice and following Him **"daily."** (Luke 9:23-24) They do this by hearing what He has had recorded in His written Word and by walking in His Holy Spirit (Psalms 33:11; 119:105; John 5:39; Acts 17:11; 2 Timothy 2:15; 3:15-16; 2 Peter 1:3-4, 20-21; Revelation 1:3; 22:18-19, etc.).

Nightfall

Proverbs 2

"My son, if thou wilt receive my words, and hide my commandments with thee; [2] So that thou incline thine ear unto wisdom, and apply thine heart to understanding; [3] Yea, if thou criest after knowledge, and liftest up thy voice for understanding; [4] If thou seekest her as silver, and searchest for her as for hid treasures; [5] Then shalt thou understand the fear of the LORD, and find the knowledge of God. [6] For the LORD giveth wisdom: out of his mouth cometh knowledge and understanding. [7] He layeth up sound wisdom for the righteous: he is a buckler to them that walk uprightly. [8] He keepeth the paths of judgment, and preserveth the way of his saints. [9] Then shalt thou understand righteousness, and judgment, and equity; yea, every good path. [10] When wisdom entereth into thine heart, and knowledge is pleasant unto thy soul; [11] Discretion shall preserve thee, understanding shall keep thee: [12] To deliver thee from the way of the evil man, from the man that speaketh froward things; [13] Who leave the paths of uprightness, to walk in the ways of darkness;

[14] Who rejoice to do evil, and delight in the frowardness of the wicked; [15] Whose ways are crooked, and they froward in their paths: [16] To deliver thee from the strange woman, even from the stranger which flattereth with her words; [17] Which forsaketh the guide of her youth, and forgetteth the covenant of her God. [18] For her house inclineth unto death, and her paths unto the dead. [19] None that go unto her return again, neither take they hold of the paths of life. [20] That thou mayest walk in the way of good men, and keep the paths of the righteous. [21] For the upright shall dwell in the land, and the perfect shall remain in it. [22] But the wicked shall be cut off from the earth, and the transgressors shall be rooted out of it." Proverbs 2:1-22

Nightfall

Prayer: *Holy Father, I want to thank You so very much for sending Your only begotten Son to die for my many sins and for the sins of the whole world. You chose to do such in the midst of our sin. Please be merciful to me, a sinner who is utterly in need of Your saving mercy and empowering, sustaining grace. Right now, if never before, I turn to You, admitting my utter poverty of spirit and bankrupt spiritual condition. I here and now fall upon Thy mercy through the blood of my LORD Jesus Christ and ask that You break me and do whatever it takes to keep my eternal soul to the end and into Your glorious eternal city! Grant my conscience, which You gave me, to be extremely sensitive to right and wrong and to Your voice – so that I can ever follow You all the way to the end and into Your eternal abode! In Jesus' holy name I pray, amen!*

CAPTURE POINTS

- In Luke 12:34-40, what is Jesus teaching? Discuss.
- According to Christ's words recorded in John 8:47, who is **"of God"** and who is **"not of God"**?
- Write out Colossians 2:8 on an index card and begin to memorize it.

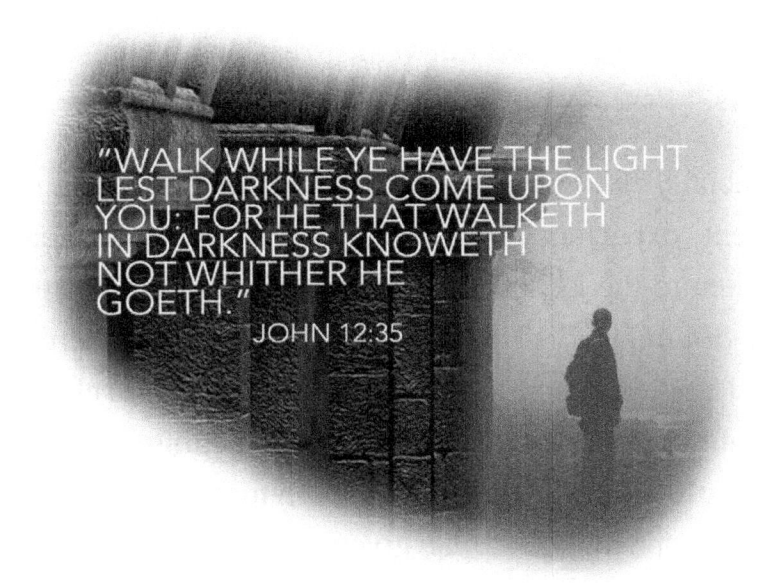

> "WALK WHILE YE HAVE THE LIGHT LEST DARKNESS COME UPON YOU: FOR HE THAT WALKETH IN DARKNESS KNOWETH NOT WHITHER HE GOETH."
> JOHN 12:35

Chapter 10

ଓଃ

What to Do If You Sin

The Answer to this Question May Shock You!

Nightfall

> **"As far as the east is from the west, so far hath he removed our transgressions from us." Psalms 103:12**

Especially in light of the soon return of Christ and our fervent expectancy of this great event, we should hearken to the LORD concerning being **"without spot, and blameless."** (2 Peter 3:14) God's Word promises that Jesus will soon return for **"a glorious church, not having spot, or wrinkle, or any such thing; but that it should be holy and without blemish."** (Ephesians 5:27) Prophetically being given a vision of the future marriage supper of the Lamb, John writes: **"Let us be glad and rejoice, and give honour to him: for the marriage of the Lamb is come, and his wife hath made herself ready. ⁸ And to her was granted that she should be arrayed in fine linen, clean and white: for the fine linen is the righteousness of saints."** (Revelation 19:7-8)

Repentance is Essential and Sin Must be Confessed

As foretold by Jude, this is a biblical truth which the OSAS (once saved always saved) and Calvinist beguilers have conveniently left out of their perverted gospel (Jude 3-4). These false teachers have perverted the grace of God, never mentioning the ongoing need to repent and confess sin as needed. Instead they perpetrate the lie of an un-conditional eternal security, promising their gullible audiences something the LORD never promised them.

The true saint of Christ will get it in his mind that Christ's salvation is conditional, not un-conditional as the false teachers claim. Man needs God and the LORD does not need man. God's Word clearly teaches us that continuing forgiveness of sins is contingent upon an abiding relationship with Christ (John 15). Such would include repentance and confession of sins as needed.

Anybody remember Jesus' parable of the ten virgins? (Matthew 25:1-13) The five wise virgins who will make it into the KING's bridal chamber (New Jerusalem) will be those who remain in vital union with Him in this life which includes repentance and remission of sin when needed (Revelation 21-22).

Anyone **"Remember Lot's wife"**? (Luke 17:32)

If forgiveness of sins was automatically applied to the born-again believer, why would God have told us that it's only when we **"confess our sins"** that He's **"faithful and just to forgive us our sins, and to cleanse us from all unrighteousness"**?

Nightfall

"If we confess our sins, he is faithful and just to forgive us our sins, and to cleanse us from all unrighteousness." 1 John 1:9

It's only those who **"walk in the light"** who remain in abiding, saving **"fellowship"** with Christ, having all sin cleansed. Their sins are cleansed because they continue to return to the LORD (repentance) as needed and confess any sin.

"But if we walk in the light, as he is in the light, we have fellowship one with another, and the blood of Jesus Christ his Son cleanseth us from all sin." 1 John 1:7

God is **"Holy, holy, holy"** and sin destroys our fellowship with Christ (Isaiah 6:3; Revelation 4:8). But once we return to Christ (when needed), confessing the sin specifically, we receive the blessed merciful forgiveness and cleansing He instantly grants.

No sin is greater than the power of the blood of Christ and so, God forbid that we allow the sin of unbelief to fill our hearts. Think about it: Just what sin is it that you committed that is greater than the cleansing power of Christ's blood? Is it not idolatry of the worst kind to place anything above **"the blood of His cross"**?

> **"In whom we have redemption through his blood, even the forgiveness of sins: ... ²⁰ And, having made peace through the blood of his cross, by him to reconcile all things unto himself; by him, I say, whether they be things in earth, or things in heaven." Colossians 1:14, 20**

Any person who has a problem with forgiveness has a serious problem with God. That's why Jesus came – to forgive the sins of the world.

> **"And she shall bring forth a son, and thou shalt call his name JESUS: for he shall save his people from their sins." Matthew 1:21**

> **"The next day John seeth Jesus coming unto him, and saith, Behold the Lamb of God, which taketh away the sin of the world." John 1:29**

> **"This is a faithful saying, and worthy of all acceptation, that Christ Jesus came into the world to save sinners; of whom I am chief." 1 Timothy 1:15**

Isn't it time we let God forgive us, that is, in our own mind? Yes, He already has forgiven you when you sincerely confessed that sin, but the problem (your lack of understanding) is with you. You see, perhaps you have not taken the LORD at His Word and simply believed what He told us. – **"If we confess our sins, HE IS FAITHFUL and just to forgive us our sins, and to cleanse us from all unrighteousness."** (1 John 1:9)

Dare we call the LORD a liar? Is that not what we do if we hesitate to believe what He plainly stated? Either He has forgiven you or He hasn't.

"Let God be true and every man a liar" beginning with you (Romans 3:4).

To those who believe that perhaps their sin was especially egregious and unforgivable, I want to ask you some simple questions:

- In light of God's **"Holy, holy, holy"** divine nature, just what sin can be committed and has been committed that He didn't send His Son to die for?
- Was our sin paid for in full by Christ on that cross or did He lie to us? (John 19:30)
- Why is *your* sin any worse than anyone else's in the eyes of a Holy God?

- Just what sin did Jesus *not* die for?
- Are we saying that God's redemption through His only begotten Son is not complete?
- If you take God's Word as true that Jesus came and died to take away your sins, how then do you somehow believe you are still guilty of anything that you've acknowledged and confessed to Him?

Hindrances to Our Having a Clean Conscience

It's clear from many Scriptures that God wants His children to have a clear conscience.

> **"Now the end of the commandment is charity out of a pure heart, and of a good conscience, and of faith unfeigned:"**
> **1 Timothy 1:5**

He wants to **"forgive us our sins"** and **"cleanse us from all unrighteousness"** and to do so thoroughly: all the way to the conscience level. See also Hebrews 9:14.

Could it be that we have not fully and completely released someone we know who committed a sin? Could that be the reason we have struggled to sense a clean, clear conscience? Perhaps if we ourselves are not freely forgiving all as God has freely forgiven us, we are reaping the difficult results of this sin (Mark 11:25-26). Could it be that if we are not showing God's mercy to others and letting them free (in our minds and attitudes), then we are hindering the blessing of a clear conscience? See Matthew 18:21-35 and James 2:13 and Matthew 7:1-5. Remember that God **"looketh on the heart"** of man (1 Samuel 16:7). Why is their sin any worse than the ones you have committed?

Those who violently oppose the ease of receiving God's forgiveness through Christ have the spirit of antichrist influencing them – because they deny Christ's redemption for works and they deny Him by disbelieving what He stated when He said: **"It is finished."** (John 19:30) **"It is finished"** means that all the sins of mankind – the whole fallen race – are "paid in full." (1 John 2:2) And Jesus taught that if we individually answer the call to be **"born again,"** we are in His kingdom and can receive forgiveness for any sin we may commit along the way.

You see, there are many who want to use your past sins (already forgiven by Jesus and confessed) against you. Therefore, to preach this forgiveness of sins by His blood is to remove the tool of control they seem to have wielded over you by holding a past sin over your head. Beware! This is witchcraft.

To combat this, we must know of a surety that Christ has completely paid for and has washed away all our sins in His blessed, precious blood.

> **"The LORD is merciful and gracious, slow to anger, and plenteous in mercy. [9] He will not always chide: neither will he keep his anger for ever. [10] He hath not dealt with us after our sins; nor rewarded us according to our iniquities. [11] For as the heaven is high above the earth, so great is his mercy toward them that fear him. [12] As far as the east is from the west, so far hath he removed our transgressions from us. [13] Like as a father pitieth his children, so the LORD pitieth them that fear him. [14] For he knoweth our frame; he remembereth that we are dust. [15] As for man, his days are as grass: as a flower of the field, so he flourisheth. [16] For the wind passeth over it, and it is gone; and the place thereof shall know it no more." Psalms 103:8-16**

The Bible tells us that sin is a choice and of our own lusts and not of God at all (James 1:13-15). Yet, God

Nightfall

made full provision for His people if they sinned after He saved them (Psalms 103:2; 1 John 1:6-2:2, etc.). The intercessory work of Christ didn't stop when He bled on that cross to pay for our sins (Hebrews 4:14-16; 7:24-26, etc.).

"In him is no sin. ⁶ Whosoever abideth in him sinneth not." 1 John 3:5-6

We know from this passage above that as we are truly abiding in Christ, we are not living in sin.

If you somehow believe that you have reached a place of sinless perfection, there is no need to read this chapter, but there is the need to read 1 John 1:8-10, Job 9:20, and Proverbs 20:9.

What should a born-again Christian do after he sins? Here's the answer: Repent (turn back to the LORD), receive God's forgiveness in confession through Jesus Christ and go help someone else! To this, some may respond with: WHAT are you talking about?! Are you crazy!? "Go do ministry?!" Really?! Are you crazy?! How can a person who recently sinned do ministry or show God's love?!

"Being justified freely by his grace through the redemption that is in Christ Jesus:

²⁵ Whom God hath set forth *to be* a propiation (atoning sacrifice) through faith in his blood, to declare his righteousness for the remission of sins that are past, through the forbearance of God." Romans 3:24-25

Remember when Peter was going to deny Christ, even with cursing, etc.? What did Jesus say for His child, Peter, to do after he had sinned and was restored back to rightful relationship with Him? Check this out:

"And the Lord said, Simon, Simon, behold, Satan hath desired to have you, that he may sift you as wheat: ³² But I have prayed for thee, that thy faith fail not: and when thou art converted, strengthen thy brethren." Luke 22:31-32

Jesus told Peter what to do after he was recovered from that fall. Note initially here that Jesus didn't instruct Peter (nor does He instruct anyone) to go do some kind of catholic penance to work off his sins and display some kind of outward work of false humility, but rather the refreshing command to **"strengthen thy brethren."** What a freedom! We are to go and pour out God's mercy to others as it has been abundantly poured out on us! Remember that one day Jesus spoke to a sinful woman and said: **"Her sins, which are many,**

Nightfall

are forgiven (freely); for she loved much: but to whom little is forgiven, the same loveth little." As we realize how much undeserved mercy has been shown to us by God, we will naturally rejoice to share this unspeakable gift with others. Our sins were/are many and His mercy is enormous and endures forever to those who fear Him (Psalms 103:11).

Here are some of the things we glean from the words of Christ in this passage (Luke 22:31-32):

- Satan seeks/desires to **"Sift you as wheat"** away from God – to cause your fellowship with God to be interrupted. This is how the devil works. Yes, there is a real devil and he hates God and you because you are the Lord's. If the leadership of your church doesn't acknowledge a real devil and a real spiritual battle that rages daily, let me encourage you to either talk to them about it or find an honest fellowship where God's Word is truly honored.

- Jesus is praying for each of His saints (YOU) – **"I have prayed for thee, that thy faith fail not"** (see also Hebrews 7:25; John 17:9).

- **"When thou art converted"**

When we sin, we are to be restored to fellowship with our LORD who loves us and has our best interests in His heart.

- **"Strengthen thy brethren"**

  Strengthen the brothers and sisters around you when you are restored – and consequently refreshed – (Acts 3:19-21). Nothing could be more important than your vital union and communion with your LORD. Rejoice in His goodness toward you! Rejoice that He has shown you mercy and ponder sharing that same mercy with others as you have received such.

- **"Freely ye have received, freely give."** (Matthew 10:8) Comfort others who have fallen or are in a season of difficulties with the comfort you have received from God (2 Corinthians 2:1-4).

- **"Ready (postured) to forgive"** Psalms 86:5, 15 say: **"For thou, Lord, art good, and ready to forgive; and plenteous in mercy unto all them that call upon thee. ... ¹⁵ But thou, O Lord, art a God full of compassion, and gracious, longsuffering, and plenteous in mercy and truth."**

Nightfall

Nothing could be more important than your vital union and communion with your Lord. Rejoice in His goodness toward you today!

Chris Sitter writes:

"I can relate to that scripture that says Satan hath desired to sift you as wheat (Luke 22:31-32). But, because of His (Christ's) mercy and blood, and longsuffering, and merciful kindness, I must share what He – in his great grace, has chosen to share with me – with His sheep. For only He, can make me accepted in the beloved. Oh, that I can share a part in the Savior's blood. A thousand hymns will not be able to capture the greatness of HIS UNSPEAKABLE GIFT! Let us press on towards the mark – one moment at a time, for there is no promise of tomorrow. Grateful for Calvary."

Wait just a minute!! What about the people who know I sinned? What will they say? What if they condemn me and call me a hypocrite because I am seeking God afresh, putting the past behind me, and serving Him by ministering His grace, love, and truth to others – after I sinned?

> **"He that spared not his own Son, but delivered him up for us all, how shall he not with him also freely give us all things?**

> ³³ **Who shall lay any thing to the charge of God's elect? It is God that justifieth.** ³⁴ **Who is he that condemneth? It is Christ that died, yea rather, that is risen again, who is even at the right hand of God, who also maketh intercession for us.** ³⁵ **Who shall separate us from the love of Christ?" Romans 8:32-35**

If the wise virgin saint lapses in his faith for some reason or the other, perhaps he shouldn't wallow in the mire of that experience, but rather repent, confess, and get right back to being about our Father's business. After Peter had sinned several times, Jesus told Him to **"Feed my sheep."** (John 21:16-17)

> **"For a just man falleth seven times, and riseth up again: but the wicked shall fall into mischief." Proverbs 24:16**

It's no time to wallow in the mire of past sins, but rather to rise up (yes again) and seek the infinitely beautiful face of the LORD. This one thing is what is needful.

> **"Seek the LORD and his strength, seek his face continually." 1 Chronicles 16:11**

Nightfall

> **"One thing have I desired of the LORD, that will I seek after; that I may dwell in the house of the LORD all the days of my life, to behold the beauty of the LORD, and to inquire in his temple." Psalms 27:4**

Origin of Righteousness

Every false religion in the world has some type of penance or asceticism (personal works or torment to earn God's forgiveness or favor). Christians stand alone, placing all of their trust and hope in the Son of God for full and complete forgiveness for all of their sin. Scores of true believers have given their lives for this vital truth, which is at the very heart of the Gospel. Jesus Christ + nothing = justification, total forgiveness, and eternal life. Now this is a good reason to verbalize our thanksgiving to our heavenly Father of this unspeakable gift! Why don't you, dear reader, take a moment to do that right now?

> **"Not by works of righteousness which we have done, but according to his mercy he saved us, by the washing of regeneration, and renewing of the Holy Ghost; [6] Which he shed on us abundantly through Jesus Christ our Saviour; [7] That being justified by his**

grace, we should be made heirs according to the hope of eternal life." Titus 3:5-7

Please allow me to strongly urge you to memorize this text above.

For the record: God is the only really holy One and we are made holy only by being in communion with Him. So, when we have truly repented, turning fully back to Him, He makes us holy again, instantly!

Friend, as a born-again believer, you may struggle within with the fleshly temptation towards doing penance – trying (after sinning) to do enough good works to somehow satisfy the claims of God's holy justice and regain His favor. No concept could be more antichrist. Nothing could strike at the heart of the Gospel more than such unbelief in the hearts of those who call themselves His children. There could be no more severe denial of the blood of Christ than this, whether one realizes it or not. This concept is a clear denial of the precious propitiatory blood of the Savior, and reveals a complete misunderstanding of the Gospel. Either Christ's blood was the full payment for all of your sins, AND/OR 1) God is a liar, 2) His whole Word (the Bible) is not true, and 3) You should immediately give up playing the part of a Christian

Nightfall

because there is no number of perfect works you can do to pay for your own sins.

> **"But we are all as an unclean thing, and all our righteousnesses are as filthy rags; and we all do fade as a leaf; and our iniquities, like the wind, have taken us away."**
> **Isaiah 64:6**

Let me encourage you to study Romans chapters 1-5 at least 7 times. Get this essential Gospel truth deep down in your heart. Pour over this text. Hi-lite, outline and cross reference it. Write down on index cards select texts the Holy Spirit puts His finger on and memorize them.

> **"As it is written, There is none righteous, no, not one." Romans 3:10**

No person can begin to understand divine forgiveness until he first understands the utterly depraved and sinful state of unredeemed men and the ultimate righteousness and sinless perfection of Christ Jesus. Listen and let your heart be blessed by this life-changing passage from Romans:

> **"Now we know that what things soever the law saith, it saith to them who are under the**

law: that every mouth may be stopped, and all the world may become guilty before God. [20] Therefore by the deeds of the law there shall no flesh be justified in his sight: for by the law is the knowledge of sin. [21] But now the righteousness of God without the law is manifested, being witnessed by the law and the prophets; [22] Even the righteousness of God which is by faith of Jesus Christ unto all and upon all them that believe: for there is no difference: [23] For all have sinned, and come short of the glory of God; [24] Being justified freely by his grace through the redemption that is in Christ Jesus: [25] Whom God hath set forth to be a propitiation through faith in his blood, to declare his righteousness for the remission of sins that are past, through the forbearance of God; [26] To declare, I say, at this time his righteousness: that he might be just, and the justifier of him which believeth in Jesus." Romans 3:19-26**

WHEW! In the Psalms, there are places where the word **"Selah"** is used to denote a place where the reader should stop and ponder or even re-read the text. I think this truth is a "Selah moment." Stop to think about it for a minute. Does this truth not vanquish the heavy and vain burden of self-righteousness? Read this last part of Romans 3 until it does. Pour over this passage until it saturates your heart, mind and thoughts.

Is our righteousness based on self-works, goodness or merit, OR the one supreme work of the Son of God? Such is a matter of life or death. Any person who leaves this earth trusting in any of their own righteousness instead of Christ's, is going to certain damnation. There is no neutral ground – **"And be found in him, not having mine own righteousness, which is of the law, but that which is through the faith of Christ, the righteousness which is of God by faith."** (Philippians 3:9)

If you are going to try to be justified by your own works, instead of relying completely upon Christ's work on the cross to make you righteous, you better not make even one slight mistake of sin:

> **"For whosoever shall keep the whole law, and yet offend in one point, he is guilty of all." James 2:10**

Saints, have we not all lusted, coveted, hated (heart murder), and committed adultery by entertaining evil thoughts? How can we repay Him? What are we going to do to merit His forgiveness and righteousness? What have we to offer the infinitely holy God of all that is? What are we in comparison to His Majesty?

We owe a debt we cannot pay
He paid a debt He did not owe

Friend, is it time for you to put away the notion or practice of self-dependence? If you are ready to repent of all traces of self-reliance and self-works for righteousness, then it is time to get excited and rejoice in the Savior who came from glory to pay the full price for all of your sins – to make you free to love and serve Him now and forever!

"Forasmuch as ye know that ye were not redeemed with corruptible things, as silver and gold, from your vain conversation received by tradition from your fathers; [19] But with the precious blood of Christ, as of a lamb without blemish and without spot." 1 Peter 1:18-19

Let's get something straight: As a believer living in this sinful world, we do not proclaim or declare our own goodness or righteousness – we have none other than what is imparted from God through Christ, the perfect One. Hello! No, rather, we declare Christ Jesus the

Nightfall

LORD, the One who said **"It is finished"**, as He drew His last breath in dying and becoming the supreme and only sacrifice for our sins and the sins of the world (John 19:30; 1 John 2:2). Yes, we **"worship God in the spirit, and rejoice in Christ Jesus, and have no confidence in the flesh."** (Philippians 3:3)

> **"And he is the propitiation (atoning sacrifice) for our sins: and not for ours only, but also for the sins of the whole world."**
> **1 John 2:2**

We should not sin again with **"an evil heart of unbelief"** by not accepting God's forgiveness through Christ who lives forever to make intercession for us at the Father's right hand (Hebrews 3:12-15, 4:14-16, 7:25). The fact is that we were never personally worthy to be forgiven in the first place, but God did such based on Christ's propitiatory sacrifice.

> **"If we confess our sins, he is faithful and just to forgive us our sins, and to cleanse us from all unrighteousness ...** [1] **My little children, these things write I unto you, that ye sin not. And if any man sin, we have an advocate with the Father, Jesus Christ the righteous:** [2] **And he is the propitiation for our sins: and**

not for ours only, but also for the sins of the whole world." 1 John 1:9; 2:1-2

Notice **"IF any man sin,"** and not "when you sin." In God's kingdom, overcoming is expected, not sinning. Yet, the LORD, through the blood of His only begotten Son, has made full provision in the whole package of the salvation He wrought through our LORD Jesus. This is the theme of the book of Hebrews.

What do you think? Do you have a testimony of forgetting those things which lie behind you and getting back up and running the race – full speed? Will you accept His mercy and forgiveness in faith without which you cannot please the LORD? (see Hebrews 11:6) Is your sin greater than Christ's divine, holy, sinless blood and the power of His divine grace to break all shackles in your life?

> **"This I recall to my mind, therefore have I hope. [22] It is of the LORD'S mercies that we are not consumed, because his compassions fail not. [23] They are new every morning: great is thy faithfulness."**
> **Lamentations 3:21-23**

Maybe something you say could strengthen another believer. The LORD truly is working and orchestrating

Nightfall

all things together for the good to those who truly love Him. In conjunction with their obedience to Him, God is conforming their lives to the image of Jesus (Romans 8:28-29).

Remember that YOU have a personal **"advocate with the Father, Jesus Christ the righteous"**, who restores your soul in the green pastures of His grace as you present yourself before Him in love. What a SAVIOR!!! What a Counselor!!! What a Shepherd!!! What a God of Restoration!!! What words could possibly do justice to His majesty?!

> **"For thou, Lord, art good, and ready to forgive; and plenteous in mercy unto all them that call upon thee ... [15] But thou, O Lord, art a God full of compassion, and gracious, longsuffering, and plenteous in mercy and truth." Psalms 86:5,15**

Jesus is coming soon, saint of the Most High. Remember to be about your Father's business so that Christ will find your hand to the plow of worshiping Him supremely and feeding His sheep, helping others come to repentance and place all their trust in **"the great Shepherd of the sheep"** (Hebrews 13:20).

Restoration is the aim of the Father. Sin is wrong because God (not men) determines what is sin – it is a violation of the holiness of the LORD (1 John 3:4). No excuse can be made for our sins (Romans 6). Yet, the past sins of others should never ever be utilized by other sinners (forgiven sinners) to manipulate or control that person. Jesus did no such thing with Peter, nor anyone else. To, in any way, use another person's sins against them is unmitigated witchcraft and actually happens in local fellowships as many of you know. If this is going on with people you are in relationship with, send them this book (or chapter) and lovingly call them to repent. If they don't, run for your life beloved (see 1 Timothy 6:3-5 KJB). Also, for more in-depth study on this topic of control, order a copy of the books *Deceivers and False Prophets Among Us* and *Predators in Our Pulpits*. Two whole chapters are dedicated to exposing the undue control of other men and its detrimental effects.

Nightfall

Prayer: *Father, in the name of my LORD and Savior Jesus Christ, please quicken my innermost being with great conviction in Thy holy fear. Unite my heart to fear Thy holy name Jesus and bless me to be quick to return to You and confess all sin as needed. My desire is to be dead so that You alone reign in this life You gave. Bless this life You gave to be one of the wise virgin saints who remain in vital fellowship with You and therefore spend eternity with You! In Jesus' name, amen.*

CAPTURE POINTS

- How important is it to understand the nothingness of **"our righteousnesses"**? Isaiah 64:6.

- Read and begin memorizing Titus 3:5-7. Perhaps read it 5 times aloud.

- Identify and discuss the divine attributes revealed in Psalms 86:5, 15.

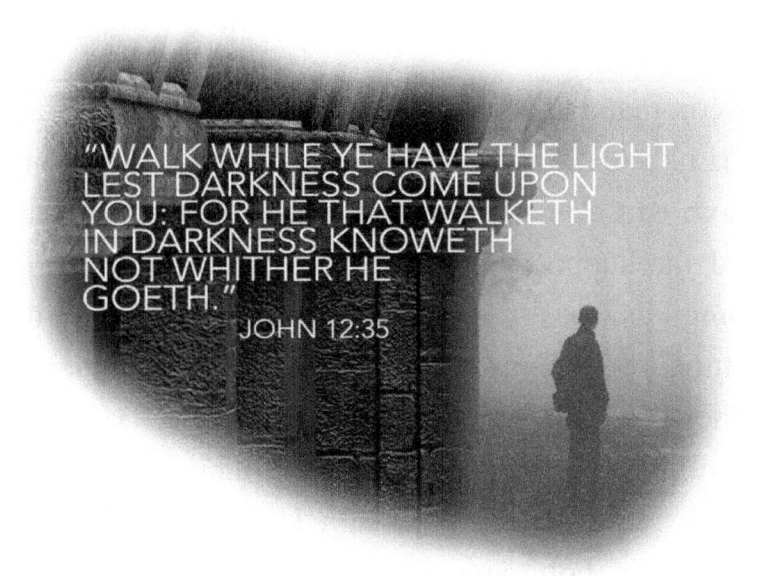

"WALK WHILE YE HAVE THE LIGHT LEST DARKNESS COME UPON YOU: FOR HE THAT WALKETH IN DARKNESS KNOWETH NOT WHITHER HE GOETH."
JOHN 12:35

Chapter 11

☙

Treasures in Heaven

Where to Give

Nightfall

**"It is more blessed to give than to receive."
Acts 20:35**

Jesus commanded us to **"give"** and promised to reward such (Luke 6:38; Acts 20:35, etc.). Yet, giving to His kingdom cause is all-important. Surely Christ will not reward the support of those ministries which are not fulfilling His Great Commission which begins with the preaching of the command and imperative to **"repent."** (Matthew 3:2; 4:17; Luke 13:3; Acts 2:38; 3:19, etc.). Any ministry that is not obeying Christ's original Gospel directives given through His own words and those of His holy apostles, is not fulfilling a New Testament purpose and should not be supported by true followers of Christ. It is of the utmost importance that we follow His edicts to be significantly rewarded both now and forevermore (Matthew 6:19-21).

First off, we should beware of self-righteous false watchmen and pastors who pat themselves on the back by saying things like "I don't take any money from the ministry. I work and make my own money." Then they spurn the pastoral watchmen who give people the opportunity to do what Jesus taught us to do – to **"give."** (Luke 6:38; Acts 20:35).

Don't buy this so fast. What they say may sound noble until you look closer at the whole counsel of God's

Word that defies such a notion and exposes these who assert such.

Did the apostle Paul and the early church take up collections? Answer: Yes. See 1 Corinthians 16:1-2. To refuse to allow God's people to give is a sin and out of the order of God established from Genesis to Revelation. In Exodus 35, God's people gave so much that the LORD had to tell them to stop. Would to God we had that problem these days. It's quite the opposite in this late hour unless you look at the masses of gullible dupes who empty their pockets on the end time wolves who are making merchandise of them (2 Peter 2:1-3).

Nearly half of Jesus' parabolic teachings deal with stewardship. Remember, in the temple, Jesus never told the Jews to remove the treasury (coffers where people have the privilege to give). No, in fact, He sat right next to it to watch how people were giving and neglecting to give (Mark 12:41-44).

Giving is instituted by the One who gave all and on record for us from Genesis to Revelation. It's the giver's privilege to give (1 Chronicles 29:14; 2 Corinthians 9:6-11; Acts 20:35). Also, God forbid that those called out by God to do His work shut up the blessing by not allowing their audience – those they

Nightfall

feed – to contribute, and thereby **"lay up"** treasure in Heaven while warding off the false god of mammon (Matthew 6:19-24).

Where we give is important.

Barry Bugh says it correctly when he writes:

"Sow ... where you see fruit. And saints, the building based local churches are not fulfilling the Great Commission our Master JESUS gave us and therefore are producing bad fruit. IN FACT, BY PARTICIPATING WITH THEM WE JOIN THEM IN REBELLION AGAINST THE LORD. As usual, as we see throughout biblical history, God is calling a remnant out from among the apostate system."

It seems that church-going people feel they need to pay their dues to the country club entertainment center they call the "church building" and its associated organization.

Are we going to be biblical? What does 1 Corinthians 9:1-14 establish? What does Galatians 6:6 and 1 Timothy 5:17-18 say? Do you know what the LORD told us for His church in these passages? Go read and get in the know – God's knowledge.

It's all in God's Word. The fact that wolves have made merchandise of the biblically illiterate, including us in the past, does nothing at all to negate or diminish aught from the clearly stated will of God. In this late hour, as the remnant is being delivered out of the deceptions of these wolves, it is not the will of God that they cease giving but rather that they re-appropriate that giving to where there is true New Testament, Great Commission fruit being born. Why should the LORD further suffer through our lives by cheating His true work out of the fuel needed? Was it His fault that we were deceived and funded false ministries in the past? This is an ugly picture, saints. Let's not abandon to abuse (throw the baby out with the bath water).

Think with me for a moment ... some love the fact that tithing is not a New Testament teaching. Why? Is it because they can now spend all their money on self? Many of them cease all giving and go back to spending all their money on the false god of self. They will spend and waste dollar on top of dollar on trash and entertainment and give little or nothing to God's work while they soothe themselves in the knowledge that tithing is not a New Testament teaching. Yet, 100% of what we receive is from God. Jesus commands us to give. What about putting God (not self) first place in every part of our lives – including stewardship of the monies He allows us to bring in?

**"Honour the LORD with thy substance, and with the first fruits of all thine increase: [10] So shall thy barns be filled with plenty, and thy presses shall burst out with new wine."
Proverbs 3:9-10**

In all things, God must be **"first"** Jesus says (Matthew 6:33; Proverbs 3:9-10).

Saints, may our LORD bless each of us to have His wisdom concerning giving back to Him. May He bless us not to lean to our own understanding, but to fully trust in what He told us in His Word (Proverbs 3:5-6).

The unchanging God will never contradict His holy Word and will only lead His children in accordance to it.

Please allow me to exhort you in the matter of your giving – according to the all-wise Counsel of the Most High.

Speaking of previously funding false prophets, one sister writes:

"Yep! Been there, done that as many have! We need to continue to give but we need to know truly where the monies are going! Investigate before you give." Darlene Troxler

Is it a sin for people doing God's work to give the ongoing opportunity for others to give/donate? No. **"And Jesus sat over against the treasury, and beheld how the people cast money into the treasury: and many that were rich cast in much."** (Mark 12:41-44) Jesus never told them to remove the treasury/coffer/place of opportunity to give. No, instead He sat right next to it to watch people giving and how they gave. He never rebuked the idea of coffers, only the misuse of them such as when He drove out the money changers (Matthew 21; John 2).

First of all, giving should be a joyful event. Our hearts should rejoice to release God's money back into His work.

> **"The LORD loveth a cheerful giver."**
> **2 Corinthians 9:7**

Our LORD tells us that all that we have comes from Him and what we give Him came from Him (1 Chron. 29:14). We will be brought into accountability before His Holy Throne of Judgment

Nightfall

concerning our stewardship of every penny He gave us and **"To whom much is given, much shall be required."** (James 4:17) We should proceed with fear and trembling in this matter. It is no small one.

Where are Christians to Give?

CONSIDER your stewardship. Is it according to biblical truth/guidelines? If you are going to honor God and thereby be rewarded by Him in your giving instead of wasting it, here are some divine directives to consider:

If you wish to plant God's resources in fertile soil, only give to true New Testament ministries that are ...

1) Teaching you the biblical imperative of death to self – the daily cross (Luke 9:23-24; Galatians 2:20, etc.),

2) Exposing OSAS for the lie from Hell that it is (Ezekiel 33:12-13; 1 Corinthians 9:27-10:12; 2 Peter 2:20-21),

3) Using the King James Bible (Psalms 12:6-7),

4) Warning you constantly (Colossians 1:28; 2:4-10, etc.),

5) Unapologetically feeding you God's pure Word (1 Peter 5:1-6),

6) Reproving, rebuking, and exhorting you (2 Timothy 4:2-4),

7) Prayerfully watching for your eternal soul (Hebrews 13:17),

8) Teaching you Jesus' truth that you must endure to the end in an abiding relationship with Him or you will be damned (Matthew 10:22; John 15:1-6,

9) Teaching you the biblical truth that Christ is coming back for a holy church that is without spot or blemish of sin (Ephesians 5:25-27; Matthew 25:1-13; Luke 21:34-36, etc.), and

10) Equipping Christ's saints for the work of the ministry (Ephesians 4:11-12).

11) Doing Christ's Great Commission as revealed at the end of each of the four Gospels.

So many times, we have all heard Christians say things like: "It doesn't matter where I give. God is going to bless me anyway. He handles the rest after I give."

BE NOT DECEIVED: God is not going to violate His own Word by blessing those who are funding His enemies. By giving to a ministry or local church that is not fulfilling Christ's Great Commission command to teach and preach His Word to saint and sinner alike, you are bidding God speed (helping, condoning) His enemies. See 2 John 7-11. To think that God doesn't watch exactly where you give – to fruit-producing or fruitless ministries – is naive and untrue.

"Bring ye all the tithes into the storehouse…" Malachi 3:8-11

His **"storehouse"** is not a physical building, but rather the place where His original Gospel is truly being obeyed and furthered in His love – where His Word of truth is being proclaimed and upheld with all boldness. 1 Peter 2:5 says the body of Christ is a **"spiritual house."** 1 Peter 5 says to **"Feed the flock of God."**

We must carefully place every dollar we give into rich Gospel soil. The LORD holds us accountable for how and where we give – and what it promotes. For the disciple of Christ, the only ministries that qualify are those which are authentically carrying out the Great Commission Christ gave – holding forth the original Gospel unwaveringly. Christ's Gospel program consists of building up the saints, preaching the Gospel and seeing people saved, water baptized, and filled with the Holy Ghost (Acts 2:37-39, 3:19, etc.). See what the early Church did in the book of Acts for a view of what the original Gospel of Christ really is. God is good.

Saints, untold thousands of Gospel workers are in lack right here and now in America. Thousands of called men of God have had to go back to their secular work due to the lack of giving among those who claim to know Christ. In the light of these facts, how can the true child of God possibly give revenues to already well-funded, secular organizations?

When we truly begin to aggrandize divine truth, we will then begin supporting only those who truly endeavor to preach all of it (full-counsel) fearlessly. We will cease from funding the ministries of hireling false prophets who allow most of their ministry revenues to be absorbed on things other than what is at the core of importance in the divine economy, like the true building up of the saints – getting them into the Word for themselves, and winning lost souls.

Concerning the work, workers and building up of God's kingdom, the Bible instructs us in Ezra 6:8 – **"forthwith expenses be given unto these men, that they be not hindered."**

The reason all of God's people are to give to His authentic work is **"that they (His servants) be not hindered."** (Ezra 6:8)

Nightfall

In judgment, the Almighty who is all-knowing and all-just is going to bring to light the pain suffered by those He called to serve Him and yet were unduly **"destitute"** (Hebrews 11:37). Today some in our midst are without basic necessities and/or funds to operate their divinely-inspired and called ministries. This is directly due to the disobedience of those who possess the ability to give to help sustain their lifestyles so they can continue to further the eternal Gospel (all get rewarded for eternity). Saints, God is going to judge us according to how we spend every dollar and punish the disobedience. Much eternal treasure remains to be laid up in your account. See 2 Corinthians 9:6-10.

Authentic, born-again saints must cease from funding worldly organizations, ministries or causes that are not divinely inspired, eternal works, according to the original Gospel. Those causes and works which align with the mission and mind of Christ are to be funded joyfully by His true disciples. They will always involve the very first Word and command of the Gospel – **"Repent: for the kingdom of heaven is at hand."** (Matthew 3:2; 4:17; Luke 13:3, 5; Acts 2:38; 3:19)

We should also refrain from supporting any entity furthering the cause of their own organization/denomination, or the leader(s). Jesus is the KING of the eternal kingdom and He alone will be reigning when all men are laid low (Isaiah 2:17-18; 42:8). In our giving, we must make certain that every dollar is used for the person in need and not absorbed into some religious bureaucracy (denominational, etc.). Of course, we must keep in mind that the Bible says in both testaments that **"the workman is worthy of his hire"** and those who do the most important work – the work of the Gospel – are to be well taken care of so they are not hindered in their work (Matthew 10:10; 1 Timothy 5:17-18).

"For where your treasure is, there will your heart be also." Matthew 6:21

His Cause

Jesus told us He came on a mission from the Father to **"seek and to save that which was lost"** (Luke 19:10), and instructed us to **"Let the dead bury their dead: but go thou and preach the kingdom of God."** (Luke 9:60) The Son of God says here plainly to *"let those that are of the world fund and further their own fleeting cause, but you my people, do all that you can to further my eternal Gospel, to rescue the perishing from eternal damnation in the lake of fire from which there will be no escape."*

"He that hath the Son hath life; and he that hath not the Son of God hath not life."
1 John 5:12

Make no mistake, there are and will be souls in Hell due to the lack of obedient and charitable giving of those today who call themselves by the name of Christ and yet disobey Him in not giving their lives and revenues to His work (Matthew 7:21). The disobedience of withholding has tied the hands of God's workers and greatly hindered their ability to do what the LORD has sent them to do in the care of souls and winning the lost.

True believers are to be possessed with the exact vision and passion of the One who came to shed His very own blood for all our sins on that wooden cross. He was raised again three days later. We are to use every possible resource He gives into our hands to further His unaltered cause – preparing men to meet Him/the care of souls. Moreover, Christ our LORD promised unending eternal rewards for every penny we give to His work in this life. He instructed us to lay up for ourselves treasure in Heaven and not on earth, and He told us that where we put our treasure is exactly where our hearts will follow and be (Matthew 6:19-21). Where one's money flows, one's heart goes.

The certain recipe for backsliding is to not give to the furtherance of God's Word. In contrast, one of the quickest ways to have a revival in your own heart is to write a check to the work of Christ. Do it now and the LORD promises to reward you.

> **"Jesus said unto him, Let the dead bury their dead: but go thou and preach the kingdom of God." Luke 9:60**

Remember, we should let the dead (unsaved) do the work of the dead – and we as the living should do the work of the living (those made alive by Christ).

> **"There is that scattereth, and yet increaseth; and there is that withholdeth more than is meet, but it tendeth to poverty. [25] The liberal soul shall be made fat: and he that watereth shall be watered also himself. [26] He that withholdeth corn, the people shall curse him: but blessing shall be upon the head of him that selleth it." Proverbs 11:24-26**

Nightfall

Prayer: *Holy Father, in the name of Jesus, please circumcise my heart and teach me Your holy ways of wisdom. Teach me to steward Your resources that You give me. Bless me to apply them correctly to bring glory to Your holy name. In Jesus' name I pray, amen.*

CAPTURE POINTS

- Did God display His loving, giving, generous, and caring divine nature by giving us His only begotten Son? John 3:16

- How important is it to give to the right ministries? What is God's standard?

- How important is it to discern which ministries are fulfilling a New Testament purpose? What are some of the New Testament purposes for ministry? Matthew 28:18-20; Mark 16:15-20; Ephesians 4:11-15, etc.

- Will those who give to ministries that are not conducting themselves according to the stated will of God be rewarded?

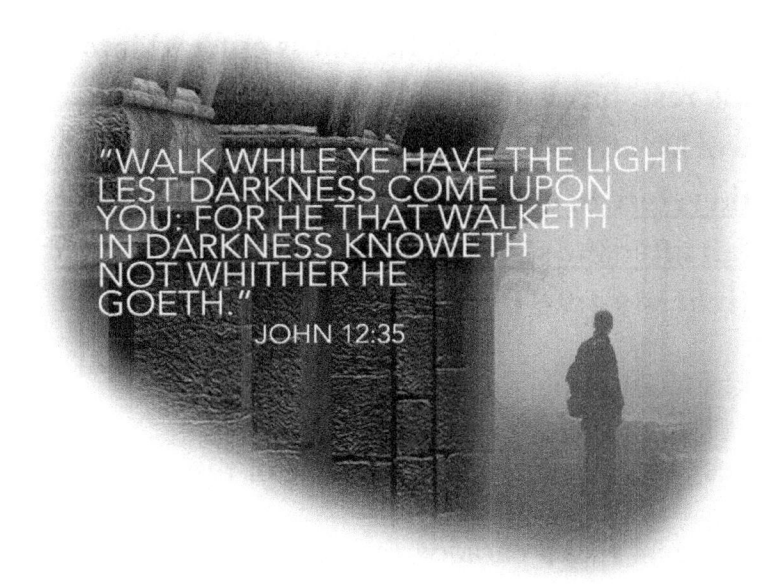

> "WALK WHILE YE HAVE THE LIGHT LEST DARKNESS COME UPON YOU: FOR HE THAT WALKETH IN DARKNESS KNOWETH NOT WHITHER HE GOETH."
> —JOHN 12:35

Chapter 12

☙❧

Be Thou Faithful unto Death

We're King's Kids but We're Not Home Yet

Nightfall

"There remaineth therefore a rest to the people of God. [10] For he that is entered into his rest, he also hath ceased from his own works, as God did from his. [11] <u>Let us labour therefore to enter into that rest, lest any man fall after the same example of unbelief.</u>" Hebrews 4:9-11

It takes labor to be able to rest.

It takes labor to remain in that place of rest.

It may seem like a paradox (contradiction) and yet, one must labor to be able to rest.

As an illustration, let's think about why a person works during the week. When a man or woman works hard all week, it's for the purpose of being able to rest at the end of his week, right? The rest is one of the reasons that he labors diligently – so that he can rest both physically and mentally. Also, people many times labor or work hard all year in order to rest for a week or two – something we call a vacation. So, they are willing to labor to enter into, and enjoy that rest, right?

In the same way, the children of God, now alive on this earth, are laboring to remain in a saving, abiding relationship with the Bridegroom in order to rest eternally with Him in the New Jerusalem and Heaven (Revelation 21-22).

The authentic disciple must **"daily"** labor or work hard and perpetually to keep Christ as his **"first love"** – his first and foremost priority (Revelation 2:4-5). That's exactly the divine purpose for the **"daily"** cross Jesus told us we must take up to truly follow Him (Luke 9:23-24).

So many have been erroneously misled and made to believe that they are unconditionally eternally secure with no further personal responsibility to truly walk with, follow, and obey the LORD and Savior who saved them.

But the Bible always links the fruit of obedience and good works to having truly repented. Genuinely repenting is surrendering one's life to the LORD. Such always yields a changed life and lifestyle.

> **"Bring forth therefore fruits meet for (consistent with) repentance: [9] And think not to say within yourselves, We have Abraham to our father (we come from a religious family heritage): for I say unto you, that God is able of these stones to raise up children unto Abraham. [10] And now also the**

axe is laid unto the root of the trees: therefore <u>every tree which bringeth not forth good fruit is hewn down, and cast into the fire.</u>" Matthew 3:8-10

"<u>Every tree</u> that bringeth not forth good fruit is hewn down, and cast into the fire." Matthew 7:19

Jesus speaks again. Here's a sampling from Revelation 2-3 which is written to the Churches, not the lost:

Those Saved Must be Faithful to Christ All the Way to Death

"Fear none of those things which thou shalt suffer: behold, the devil shall cast some of you into prison, that ye may be tried; and ye shall have tribulation ten days: be thou faithful unto death, and I will give thee a crown of life." Revelation 2:10

"And he that overcometh, and keepeth my works unto the end, to him will I give power over the nations." Revelation 2:26

"He that overcometh, the same shall be clothed in white raiment; and I will not blot out his name out of the book of life, but I will

confess his name before my Father, and before his angels." Revelation 3:5

Those who cling to Christ will be blessed to be in that New Jerusalem with Him and the Father! (Revelation 21)

"He shall enter into peace: they shall rest in their beds, each one walking in his uprightness." Isaiah 57:2

"And I heard a voice from heaven saying unto me, Write, Blessed are the dead which die in the Lord from henceforth: Yea, saith the Spirit, that they may rest from their labours; and their works do follow them." Revelation 14:13

What most don't stop to realize is that most pastors want them to feel good so that they keep coming to and patronizing the pastor's church social club business (franchise) he's set up. So, to catch souls who will come and then be repeat customers, they do not want you to know the hard truths of the Bible. So, they sell you on a false gospel that requires nothing from you. They are peddling you right into Hell. Only the biblically illiterate – those who refuse to know God and therefore His Word for themselves – are going to be destroyed.

"My people are destroyed for lack of knowledge." Hosea 4:6

There are many things in this world that distract us from pure worship of the LORD and that's the reason there is hard work involved to rest at His feet.

"Let us labour therefore to enter into that rest, lest any man fall after the same example of unbelief." Hebrews 4:11

Labor doesn't always equal physically hard work. No, labor many times simply means doing the right thing, just like Mary did when she sat at Jesus' feet and listened to Him speak His Word. Christ told her that she chose **"that good part."** He made it clear that *worshiping* Him was more important than *working* for Him. God's not much interested in our *work* for Him if we are not truly *worshiping* Him in spirit and in truth (John 4:23-24). These things are plainly communicated to us by Jesus right here in His words to Mary and Martha.

"Now it came to pass, as they went, that he entered into a certain village: and a certain

woman named Martha received him into her house. ³⁹ And she had a sister called Mary, which also sat at Jesus' feet, and heard his word. ⁴⁰ But <u>Martha was cumbered about much serving</u>, and came to him, and said, Lord, dost thou not care that my sister hath left me to serve alone? bid her therefore that she help me. ⁴¹ And Jesus answered and said unto her, Martha, Martha, thou art careful and troubled about many things: ⁴² But <u>one thing is needful: and Mary hath chosen that good part, which shall not be taken away from her</u>." Luke 10:38-42**

Note that to Martha, who was too busy to sit and worship Him, Jesus says **"Martha, Martha, thou art careful and troubled about many things."** Could Jesus be saying to you as He said to Martha, "(<u>your name</u>, <u>your name</u>), **thou art careful and troubled about many things"**?

Are you too busy to sit and worship, to seek, and to go deeper with Christ?

Is your life so busy with temporal things that you have no time or desire for the eternal God who came and died to save your soul to have real fellowship with you?

Nightfall

Does your empty heart long to be filled, anchored, settled, and sound in an intimate relationship with the Savior? We were designed for just this and so if it's not happening in our lives, we are empty, no matter what else we appear to have going for us.

Like Martha, many of us are 'running and gunning' as the saying goes. Our lives are in disarray, in a whirlwind. We are hollow, void, empty. We run to and fro and yet are empty inside because of our lack of true, intimate fellowship with the LORD Jesus. Nothing's going to change until we turn back to Him.

God works from the inside out in His relationship with man and that life with Christ is nurtured by daily intimate communion with Him. Many things in Scripture teach us that the LORD works on the inside first, including the fact that Christ rebuked the Pharisee religionists of His day because they tended only to the outer man but not the inner life of the man (Matthew 23).

The stated reason the LORD created man was for fellowship with Him.

> **"And let them make me a sanctuary; that I may dwell among them (fellowship with them)." Exodus 25:8**

> **"And this is life eternal (the chief purpose for it), <u>that they might know thee</u> the only true God, and Jesus Christ, whom thou hast sent." John 17:3**

The apostle Paul's superseding, dominant, prevailing, and overriding life goal was to know Christ more and more – better and better. This was the **"mark"** (bull's eye) he relentlessly pressed toward:

> **"<u>That I may know him</u>, and the power of his resurrection, and the fellowship of his sufferings, being made conformable unto his death." Philippians 3:10**

Knowing Christ requires suffering death to self and being conformed to his death where you die so He can live and reign in your life.

Knowing Jesus better was Paul's **"prize"** or ultimate award:

> **"Brethren, I count not myself to have apprehended: but this one thing I do, forgetting those things which are behind, and reaching forth unto those things which are before, [14] I press toward the mark for the**

prize (award) of the high calling of God in Christ Jesus." Philippians 3:13-14

The award or **"prize"** of the believer, brought into God's kingdom family, is to **"know Him."**

Being Still to Know Him

Many times, laboring to rest in Christ takes much work to be set apart to escape all the activities and distractions of this sinful world that keep us from pressing deeper into fellowship with Him.

> **"Be still, and know that I am God: I will be exalted among the heathen, I will be exalted in the earth." Psalms 46:10**

Either Christ will emerge and reign in our lives among the heathen or their bustling, lustful activities will.

> **"And the world passeth away (temporal), and the lust thereof: but he that doeth the will of God abideth for ever." 1 John 2:17**

Getting to know Jesus better is doing **"the will of the Father."** In fact, nothing could please God more.

He saved us and so why do we spend or squander most of our focus, time, energies, and effort chasing happiness or money in this world system that is going to be soon vanquished forever?

The goal of every disciple of Jesus should be greater intimacy with Him. That takes labor and is why God's Word instructs us to **"labour therefore to enter into that rest, lest any man fall after the same example of unbelief."** (Hebrews 4:11)

There's a warning in this too – **"lest any man fall after the same example of unbelief."** In other words, anyone who doesn't labor to rest in Christ will fall into unbelief.

Unbelief for a believer? Yes, if he neglects intimate fellowship with Jesus.

> **"How shall we escape (eternal judgment), if we neglect so great salvation; which at the first began to be spoken by the Lord, and was confirmed unto us by them that heard him ... holy brethren ... Take heed, brethren, lest there be in any of you an evil heart of unbelief, in departing from the living God. [13] But exhort one another daily, while it is called To day; lest any of you be hardened through the deceitfulness of sin. [14] For we are made partakers of Christ, if we**

Nightfall

hold the beginning of our confidence stedfast unto the end." Hebrews 2:3; 3:1, 12-14

In this above passage, as is the case throughout Scripture, the erroneous notion is shattered that one who is truly saved is safe and secure unconditionally. Satan is a liar and the father and peddler of this profuse propaganda and falsehood.

Jesus warns us of things that draw us away from Him and cause us to be unfruitful, choked, and fall away if they are not dealt with and cut out of our lives.

"And these are they which are sown among thorns; such as hear the word, [19] And the cares of this world, and the deceitfulness of riches, and the lusts of other things entering in, choke the word, and it becometh unfruitful." Mark 4:18-20

Jesus teaches here that **"the cares of this world, and the deceitfulness of riches, and the lusts of other things"** are the things that if allowed, **"choke the word (in our lives), and it becometh unfruitful."** So, because of these things, God's Word becomes null and void in us – it ceases to have fertile ground in which to grow. When we lust after things other than more of Christ, His Word ceases to have root in us. It ceases to germinate, thrive, or flourish in our hearts and lives. Those things, if allowed, make His Word of none effect in us. **"The seed is the word of God"** and is perfect – **"incorruptible"** – but the ground it's planted in determines the fruit born (Luke 8:11; 1 Peter 1:23). All growth and life will cease if we don't labor to evade these things Jesus warned us of – to rid our hearts and lives of them. What are they again?

- **"the cares of this world,"** – busy-ness
- **"and the deceitfulness of riches,"** – lust for power via temporary wealth, greed, covetousness, idolatry
- **"the lusts of other things"** – entanglements due to not seeking the LORD's face and putting Him first

Any one of these things will cancel the vital, life-giving power and influence of God's Word in us.

There's no question that God's Word never returns to him void but always accomplishes His will. His Word, which is given to us all, either accomplishes salvation and divine life in us or if we choose to neglect it and not hear and obey it, such will be a testimony against us in that day for having set it aside for things that we chose to count more important to us than Him.

> "Whoso despiseth the word shall be destroyed: but he that feareth the commandment shall be rewarded."
> Proverbs 13:13

The Jews were first given and yet chose to reject their Messiah and His saving Word of truth.

> "Then Paul and Barnabas waxed bold, and said, It was necessary that the word of God should first have been spoken to you (the Jews): but <u>seeing ye put it from you, and judge yourselves unworthy of everlasting life</u>, lo, we turn to the Gentiles." Acts 13:46

Those who do not take God's Word seriously enough to obey His instructions to them are putting it from them and counting themselves **"unworthy of everlasting life"** with Him.

It Comes Down to Who We Choose to Love Supremely

> "Jesus said unto him, <u>Thou shalt love the Lord</u> thy God with all thy heart, and with all thy soul, and with all thy mind. [38] This is the first and great commandment. [39] And the

second is like unto it, Thou shalt love thy neighbour as thyself." Matthew 22:37-39

We are to love the LORD our God with all our heart affection, soul, and mind and, therefore, to love not this sinful world which would cause us to forfeit our relationship with the LORD.

It's impossible to love both.

It's impossible to serve more than one supreme master.

The LORD has set things up so that one must choose.

Here's God's ultimatum:

> **"For where your treasure is, there will your heart be also. [22] The light of the body is the eye (dependent on the vision/focus): if therefore thine eye (vision) be single (singly focused), thy whole body shall be full of light. [23] But if thine eye (focus) be evil, thy whole body shall be full of darkness. If therefore the light that is in thee be darkness, how great is that darkness! [24] <u>No man can serve two masters: for either he will hate the one, and love the other; or else he will hold to the one, and despise the other.</u>**

<u>Ye cannot serve God and mammon."</u>
Matthew 6:21-24

One cannot be purely focused on money and the Master simultaneously. The life that has Christ as its treasure (first priority, first love) is flooded daily with His life, light, and love. Among the many who claim to be saved today, it's all too rare to meet someone who is full of Christ – fully immersed in His Holy Spirit and, therefore, beaming with His life, love, and truth. Every true follower of Christ should be emptied of self and full of the Savior who is **"the truth," "the light of the world,"** and who **"is love."** (John 14:6; 8:12; 1 John 4:8) Jesus told us to **"Let your light so shine before men, that they may see your good works, and glorify your Father which is in heaven."** (Matthew 5:16) It is clear that the divine intention is that the light of Christ who is the light of the world should be shining – beaming – from the lives of every one of His people.

Where is your treasure? In other words, what do you value most? Is Christ your true treasure? Do you long to know Him better? Is He your all-consuming focus?

If we genuinely wish to assess and discover what the true priority of our lives is, we must simply examine whom or what we are seeking.

> **"Seek the LORD and his strength, seek his face continually." 1 Chronicles 16:11**
>
> **"Now set (affix) your heart and your soul to seek the LORD your God." 1 Samuel 22:19**

The life that has no resting place – resting in the LORD – is out of control. Being anchored in Christ, our **"exceeding great reward,"** requires a deliberate choice to truly surrender to and to make Jesus Christ our **"first love."** (Genesis 15:1; Revelation 2:4-5)

Repent and Turn Back to Me

Jesus complimented the church at Ephesus and then sought to correct them. After congratulating this church on things done well, Christ says:

> **"Nevertheless I have somewhat against thee, because <u>thou hast left thy first love</u>.** [5] **Remember therefore from whence thou art fallen, and repent, and do the first works; or else I will come unto thee quickly, and will remove thy candlestick out of his place, except thou repent." Revelation 2:4-5**

Does Jesus have anything **"against"** you? If so, would you want to know it so you could correct it? He told these believers that they needed to **"repent"** and turn

Nightfall

again to Him because He said, **"thou hast left thy first love."** Make no mistake, Jesus had this **"against"** them. Does He have this **"against"** you?

Christ instructed them to return to Him – **"Remember therefore from whence thou art fallen, and repent."** They had backslidden from the rightful place of having Him first in their lives in the past and He was calling them back to Himself.

To make Christ our **"first love"** is to repent of idolatry and put Him first in our lives. Only the LORD Jesus Christ is worthy to be **"first"** in our lives. He alone is worthy to be loved, celebrated, magnified, praised, worship, thanked and obeyed.

Idolatry is sin – soul-damning sin.

> **"Thou shalt have no other gods before me." Exodus 20:3**

> **"For thou shalt worship no other god: for the LORD, whose name is Jealous, is a jealous God." Exodus 34:14**

> **"But the fearful (timid, cowardly), and unbelieving, and the abominable, and murderers, and whoremongers, and sorcerers, and <u>idolaters</u>, and all liars, shall**

have their part in the lake which burneth with fire and brimstone: which is the second death." Revelation 21:8

Is the LORD Jesus Christ important to you?

Is there anything else more important to you?

God wants our focused, undivided attention. He requires that He be the first priority of our lives and no other. The LORD is a jealous God and wants His child to be singly focused upon knowing and pleasing Him. Everything else in that life will be blessed.

"But seek ye first the kingdom of God, and his righteousness; and all these things shall be added unto you." Matthew 6:33

In this context, what did Jesus mean? What was He speaking of in that discourse? He was speaking of food, drink, clothing, shelter, and your life. And He was saying to put Him first and all the other things of this life – necessities – will be given to you. In other words, "I am going to take good care of you and your needs and your family and yet, I want you to focus upon and to seek Me, not those things."

Competition

There are things in this life that compete for our attention and heart affections. On this Earth there's always going to be competition or things vying for our attention – to draw away from pure and prioritized devotion to Christ. This is a test to see who is first place in our lives. Our supreme love for the LORD instead of self proves He alone stands as our priority – our **"first love."** (Revelation 2:4-5)

> **"Love not the world, neither the things that are in the world. If any man love the world, the love of the Father is not in him.** [16] **For all that is in the world, the lust of the flesh, and the lust of the eyes, and the pride of life, is not of the Father, but is of the world.** [17] **And the world passeth away, and the lust thereof: but he that doeth the will of God abideth for ever." 1 John 2:15-17**

The life that is rooted in knowing Christ is bountifully fruitful for His eternal glory.

> **"And these are they which are sown on good ground; such as hear the word, and receive it, and bring forth fruit, some thirtyfold, some sixty, and some an hundred."**
> **Mark 4:20**

Prayer: *LORD, I have sinned against Thee in not putting You supremely first place in my personal life. More now than ever, I recognize that this is vile sin. I am guilty before You and now, this moment come to You in repentance, asking You to please forgive me for not putting You first. You alone are worthy to be first – to be reigning – in my heart and life. At this moment, I turn to You fully, laying my life in Your holy hands. Into Your hands I now submit my spirit, soul, and body in worship to You. LORD Jesus, I must admit that I have a deep fear that somehow I could fall away, so I ask you to do whatever is necessary to prepare me – to imbue me – with Your holy fear so that I would never deny You but rather confess and worship You alone to the end, no matter what the cost. I want You now and I want to be with You forever! Please forgive my sins and wash me clear and clean in the precious blood of Jesus Christ. LORD Jesus, please now cleanse me and fill me to worship and to please You in all things. In Jesus' holy name I pray, amen.*

CAPTURE POINTS

- What three things did Christ tell us choke His Word out of our lives and cause us to be ungrounded and unfruitful? See Mark 4:18-20.
- Read and begin memorizing Jesus' words on record for us in Matthew 6:33. Perhaps read it five times aloud. Write it down on an index card.
- Read and discuss 1 John 2:15-17. Identify the three things the Holy Spirit tells us draw us away from Christ.

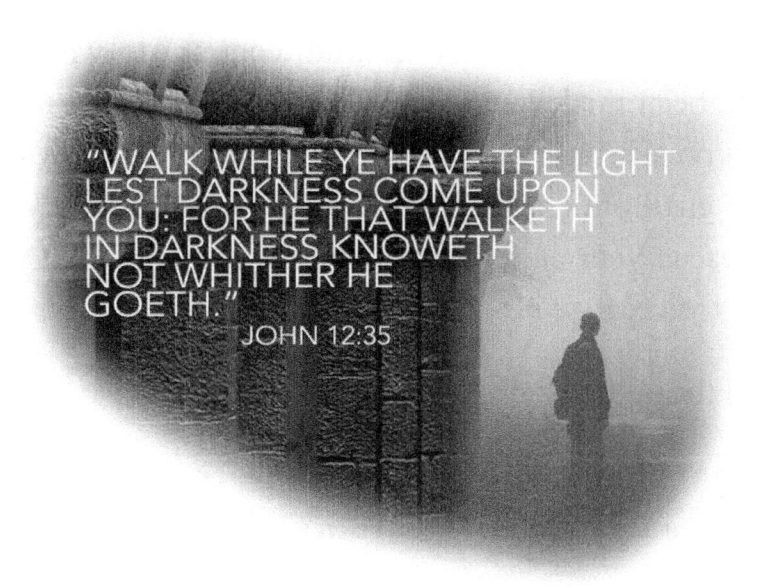

"WALK WHILE YE HAVE THE LIGHT LEST DARKNESS COME UPON YOU: FOR HE THAT WALKETH IN DARKNESS KNOWETH NOT WHITHER HE GOETH."
JOHN 12:35

Chapter 13

☙

Don't Miss this Divine Prescription for Blessing

Are those who speak the raw truth of God's Word "negative" people or is the truth contrary to what we have been misled/conditioned to believe? Could those who preach the truth, the full-counsel of God's Word, be a gift from God to you? Could the LORD be trying to rescue your eternal soul before it's too late and you don't yet realize it?

Paul the apostle said:

> **"Am I therefore become your enemy, because I tell you the truth?" Galatians 4:16**

Even an amateur Bible student realizes that God's prophets and apostles – those true messengers of His – were despised, rejected and murdered by the religious hypocrites of their day. Could it be that you are just like those Hell bound hypocrites? Do you attack those who preach sin, repentance, and the danger of eternal Hell?

Why Does Jesus Save Souls?

> **"Who gave himself for us, THAT he might redeem us from all iniquity, and purify unto himself a peculiar people, zealous of good works." Titus 2:14**

Does Jesus save a soul just to bless him with trinkets in this fleeting world of which He said His kingdom is not of? (John 18:36) Why does Jesus save a person? Is it just for that person to live a life of self-serving pursuits and lusts? For what purpose does the LORD save someone?

> **"And as they were eating, <u>Jesus took bread, and blessed it, and brake it</u>, and gave it to the disciples, and said, Take, eat; this is my body." Matthew 26:26**

As He did with this bread, it seems that He blesses us with His salvation and then breaks us to be used of Him in reaching the world around us. That's quite a differing picture from that being painted by the vast majority of church leaders today.

Like it or not, the bad news must come before the Good News. Don't like it? Tough! Deal with things GOD's way or perish as a lawless **"worker of iniquity."** (Matthew 7:21-23) The lake of fire awaits!

> **"But when he saw many of the Pharisees and Sadducees (those who claim to know God) come to his baptism, he said unto them, O generation of vipers, who hath warned you to flee from the wrath to come? [8] Bring forth**

> **therefore fruits meet for repentance: ⁹ And think not to say within yourselves, We have Abraham to our father ("I'm a Baptist, I was saved at 12," etc.): for I say unto you, that God is able of these stones to raise up children unto Abraham. ¹⁰ And now also the axe is laid unto the root of the trees: therefore every tree which bringeth not forth good fruit is hewn down, and cast into the fire." Matthew 3:7-10**

No breakthrough will ever occur in the life of the person who is a moral coward and refuses to submit to the sanctifying, breaking, rebuking, and killing process. That person who would naysay to the messengers of the LORD is in darkness and loves his/her darkness and is, therefore, not coming to the light (John 3:19-21). They shall never see or understand or walk in the LORD's blessed grace until they are truly humble and die to self and submit to His Word (James 4:6-10).

> **"He that covereth (tries to hide) his sins shall not prosper: but whoso confesseth and forsaketh them shall have mercy." Proverbs 28:13**

If you don't want HIS "negative," you will not receive His blessings and that's positive!

Perhaps the problem is that we don't yet understand that God's kingdom is all about King Jesus and so it doesn't revolve around us but rather Him.

Who's the potter of your life? You or God?

Jeremiah 18:6 says **"O house of Israel, cannot I do with you as this potter? saith the LORD. Behold, as the clay is in the potter's hand, so are ye in mine hand, O house of Israel."**

May God grant us hearts of flesh, making us humble, pliable, and teachable (Ezekiel 36:24-26).

Divine Prescription for Blessing

Okay, read this verse closely and see what comes first in God's economy for us, the negative or the positive? Look for and find the six elements of renovation required by God and note the divine order:

> **"See, I have this day set thee over the nations and over the kingdoms, to root out, and to pull down, and to destroy, and to throw down, to build, and to plant." Jeremiah 1:10**
>
> 1. **"to root out"**
>
> 2. **"to pull down"**

Nightfall

3. **"to destroy"**

4. **"to throw down"**

5. **"to build"**

6. **"to plant"**

The LORD is working in His children **"to root out"** and **"to pull down"** and **"to destroy"** and **"to throw down"** all false perceptions, notions, and beliefs of Him so that He can begin **"to build"** and **"to plant"** that which is His truth in us.

Why would this simple order and process given to us by God be hard to understand? Do you let your children eat the dessert first or the meat and vegetable? Do you wax your floor or car first or do you CLEAN it first and then wax it? Do you use mouthwash first or do you brush your teeth clean first?

Many who are either simply very immature spiritually, and or those who are waxing cold in this late hour, do not **"endure sound doctrine"** and so reject the "negative" communication involved in transmitting the full counsel of God's Word.

In Hebrews 12:24-28, we are told that God is shaking all things and those who are not submitting to Him and

His process of being conformed to the holy image of the Son of God, are being ousted as bad fruit from the tree of His eternal kingdom. They are not remaining in Him and, therefore, will be cast into the fires of eternal damnation (John 15:1-6).

These who reject the message of repentance and sanctification will never experience **"times of refreshing ... from the presence of the LORD"** because they are in rebellion, refusing to do things God's way. No, instead they are foolishly attempting to come to and serve God on their own terms. **"The presence of the LORD"** and **"refreshing"** are only known to those who are presently submitting to God – on HIS terms. There will be no blessing for the wicked who rebel – now or ever (Psalms 68:6b).

Notice in the following verse how God desires to refresh the soul of the righteous and yet repentance must, of necessity, precede that blessed breakthrough:

> **"<u>Repent</u> ye therefore, and be converted, that your sins may be blotted out, when the times of <u>refreshing</u> shall come from the presence of the Lord." Acts 3:19**

Those who reject the "negative" message of repentance and God calling out our sins define themselves as the exact ones who need this message. To those who are right with God, to those who love Him more than themselves, his commandments are not grievous.

"For this is the love of God, that we keep his commandments: and his commandments are not grievous." 1 John 5:3

It's ALWAYS a matter of just WHO we love most – God or self.

There are two kinds of people who claim to be Christ's – the proud and the humble:

"God resisteth (sets Himself against) the proud but giveth grace to the humble." James 4:6

But the LORD is not working in many who refuse to hold themselves accountable to **"sound doctrine"** but rather heap false teachers to themselves that never preach the negative stuff that is totally necessary. This is exactly why seeker-friendly, emergent church devils, and people like Rick Warren, and Joel Osteen are so popular today. These smiling wolves are flattering you straight into the bowels of eternal damnation. Hell awaits. These ravenous beguilers tickle the ears of people for their own self-serving "success," catering to what they know self-loving people want to hear. It's a business strategy and it's for your very soul. They are literally fulfilling prophecy:

> **"Preach the word; be instant in season, out of season; reprove, rebuke, exhort with all long suffering and doctrine. ³ For the time will come when <u>they will not endure sound doctrine</u>; but after their own lusts shall they heap to themselves teachers, having itching ears; ⁴ And they shall turn away their ears from the truth, and shall be turned unto fables." 2 Timothy 4:2-4**

Does anyone want to argue with the ALMIGHTY? Beloved, JUST WHAT did He list first? Get to know what our LORD told us in Jeremiah 1:10. You will need it often/daily due to the innumerable lost souls who think they are saved, but listen to spineless moral cowards today who fill the media telling people what THEY – their sinful flesh – want to hear.

This is the Gospel. Death and burial must precede resurrection and only those who submit to and endure the death will experience the resurrection. It's how things work between a Holy God and sinful men. John the Baptist had to come before Christ to **"prepare ye the way of the LORD."** (Isaiah 40:3-5) Just like all

Old Testament prophets, John the Baptist's preaching totally cited the sin of God's people and called them to repent or perish (Matthew 3:7-10). This is necessary to restore a life. The old must be done away with. **"New wine MUST be put into new bottles."** (Mark 2:22)

> **"The voice of him that crieth in the wilderness, Prepare ye the way of the LORD, make straight in the desert a highway for our God. [4] Every valley shall be exalted, and every mountain and hill shall be made low: and the crooked shall be made straight, and the rough places plain: [5] And the glory of the LORD shall be revealed, and all flesh shall see it together: for the mouth of the LORD hath spoken it." Isaiah 40:3-4**

Prayer: *LORD, I ask You to place this truth deeply into my heart so that I can love people as You love me. Let me love them enough to relate to and speak to them keeping in mind the truth of their eternal destination. Give me enough compassion for their souls that I will have the love and courage to tell them about the reality of Hell as well as the good news of the Gospel and Your Precious Son, Jesus. Please bless me to submit more wholeheartedly to the process of dying to self so that Your life will reign supreme in this vessel. Father, as the darkness of this world increases, please bless me to be humble and honest toward Your Word and truth so that I can be light and salt bringing many into Your kingdom. "Even so, come, Lord Jesus."*

CAPTURE POINTS

- Closely read Jeremiah 1:10 and discuss the divine pattern and principle revealed.

- Discuss the reasons a person would view God's instructions/commandments as being drudgery or a joy. See 1 John 5:3.

- Who does God resist? Who does He come near to and exalt? Read James 4:6-10. Begin memorizing this passage.

Addendum

☙

Making Peace with God

Are You Ready to Pass from Death to Life?

The most astounding event of human history occurred when this man, Jesus Christ, died on a Roman cross. When He died, an untimely darkness covered the land at 3:00 p.m. and an earthquake occurred as He took His final breath. This man called Jesus was crucified. Three days later He was raised from the dead! Here's why He died:

> **"But your iniquities (sins) have separated between you and your God, and your sins have hid his face from you, that he will not hear." Isaiah 59:2**

God is holy and our sins separate us from Him. We have all broken God's laws by lying, dishonoring our parents, cheating, hating, committing a sex act in our mind with someone we are not married to, stealing,

Nightfall

coveting, taking His holy name in vain, etc. These are all sins against God and we are all guilty. Committing any single one of these sins makes us guilty of breaking the whole law and worthy of death.

Divine justice demands that our violations be punished. Because we are guilty of breaking God's holy law, we deserve to be fairly repaid for our offenses. God doesn't want us to be punished in Hell forever though, so He sent His Son to pay the debt for us, so we would not have to pay for our own sins in eternal Hell as we clearly deserve, but rather live now and forever with Him. What love!

At the end of a perfect (sinless) life, Christ carried the very cross He was to be nailed to. His infinite love for you, along with the nails driven through His hands and feet, held Him to that cross as He agonized for 6 hours in pain – to pay for your sins. He was crucified to make peace between God and man. The Son of God bridged the gap that sin had caused. This wonderful man named Jesus chose to shed His life blood (die – in excruciating pain) for you rather than live without you. He loves you.

> **"For the wages of sin is death; but the gift of God is eternal life through Jesus Christ our Lord." Romans 6:23**

Christ died to fully pay for the sins of the human race (John 19:30). God loves us and wants us to experience relationship with Him, now and forever (John 17:3). Friend, who else has ever died for you but Jesus, the Good Shepherd?

> **"For when we were yet without strength, in due time Christ died for the ungodly (that's you)." Romans 5:6**

> **"Christ Jesus came into the world to save (rescue) sinners." 1 Timothy 1:15**

No religion or religious figure can save your soul from Hell (no matter what they claim). Jesus didn't come to start a religion but rather to establish His eternal kingdom in the hearts of men, granting them a relationship with God. Jesus Christ is the only One who bears nail-scarred hands and feet for your sins. He is the only way to God and your only hope.

> **"For there is ONE God, and ONE mediator between God and men, the man Christ Jesus." 1 Timothy 2:5**

The Son of God died and rose again to take away all your sins. He was the only One qualified for the job and He is the only One worthy of your worship.

Nightfall

Peace with God Happens When We Meet the Prince of Peace

It is by no accident you are reading this message. This is your moment in history to be saved. Praying and doing good deeds and going to church will save no person from eternal punishment – **"For by grace (undeserved favor) are ye saved through faith; and that not of yourselves: it is the gift of God: Not of works, lest any man should boast."** (Ephesians 2:8-9) Only the good work of Christ shedding His sinless blood on the cross for you will save your soul as you repent before a holy and righteous God and Judge. If you are going to get right with the LORD and go to Heaven, there must be a moment of reckoning. Now is your time to be saved. No one will ever through a life of good works earn God's favor. There must, of necessity, be that divinely-defining moment when you lay your whole life/being/existence into His perfect, holy hands.

Apply His holy blood to your life so that you may be saved, forgiven, and live eternally with Him. You must completely turn your life over to Him in repentance and faith.

In a moment of sincere solitude, get alone with God or pray with another true born-again Christian or by yourself. Take yourself away from all else to honor the One who made you, bowing your heart to speak in prayer with Him who is Your God and Judge. He is listening. In fact, He's the very One who orchestrated all of this and brought you to this place.

Below is a model prayer. If you will pray to God sincerely and from the depths of your heart, in sincere repentance in turning to the LORD with all that is in you, the LORD will hear and answer your prayer and save you.

Your Prayer of Repentance to God to Be Saved

Heavenly Father, right now if never before, I come before You as a sinner, fully admitting that I have sinned against You in many ways and am guilty and worthy of Your wrath. I wish to settle out of court before it's too late and thank You for making full provision for me to do just that. I here and now denounce all trust in my own goodness, good works, or religion of any kind. I am here now and repenting. I turn my whole being and life over to You right now. I am not worthy of Your mercy but You sent Your only begotten Son Jesus Christ to die—to shed His blood—for my sins on that cross. After He was buried for three days You raised my LORD from the dead whereby You made the only way for me to know You! Thank You, Holy Father! I now confess Jesus Christ as my LORD and Savior and believe You raised Him from the dead to justify me. I beg You to take over my life LORD Jesus. Please fill me with Your Holy Spirit. Lead me into the way everlasting! I love You, Jesus, and thank You for finding and saving me! From this moment forward, I will serve You. I will tell others about Your great love and how You want to save them too! In Jesus' name, amen!

What Now?

Tell another Christian. Find a group of Christ-loving, Bible-living believers. Be water baptized. Read your King James Bible daily and talk with God in prayer. Follow Christ to the end of your life.

- Give Him thanks. Preferably with uplifted heart and hands, give forthright, verbal thanksgiving to the LORD daily for finding and saving you from sin and Hell and for His glory and eternal purpose.
- Ask the LORD to fill you with His Holy Spirit (Acts 1:4-8; 2:14; 2:38-39; 19:1-6).

- Tell another Christian that the LORD has saved you (Luke 12:8 -9).
- Find a group of Christ-centered believers who love God's Word and study it unceasingly. Stay clear of those who are proud of their church, their pastor, or their denomination. Fellowship with those who unceasingly magnify Jesus Christ, the nail scarred risen Savior above all else (Colossians 2).
- Be water baptized (Acts 2:38).
- Obtain a copy of the booklet titled *What to do Now that He Has Saved You!* available on SafeGuardYourSoul.com.
- Read your King James Bible daily and talk with God in prayer. Read at least four chapters every morning as soon as you awake.
- Follow Christ to the end of your life (Matthew 24:13).
- Read and obey God's Word (James 1:22).
- Read articles, listen to audios, etc., and sign up for the free email devotional at SafeGuardYourSoul.com to help you to grow in grace as a born-again disciple of Jesus (Colossians 2:6-10).
- Get your supply of soul-winning Gospel tracts and copies of this book to share with others.

See All Current Resources Here:

SafeGuardYourSoul.com

Sharpening Your

Personal Discernment

For the Building up of His Saints

SafeGuardYourSoul.com

GreatCommissionAdventure.com

Let's grow together! Sign up here to begin receiving the Moments with Our Master email devotional that is sure to help you grow in His grace and in the knowledge of our LORD and Savior Jesus Christ (2 Peter 1:2; 3:18). It's sent out once or twice weekly for the edification of the body of Christ in this late hour. Sign up at <u>info@SafeGuardYourSoul.com</u>

SafeGuardYourSoul.com

GreatCommissionAdventure.com

Nightfall

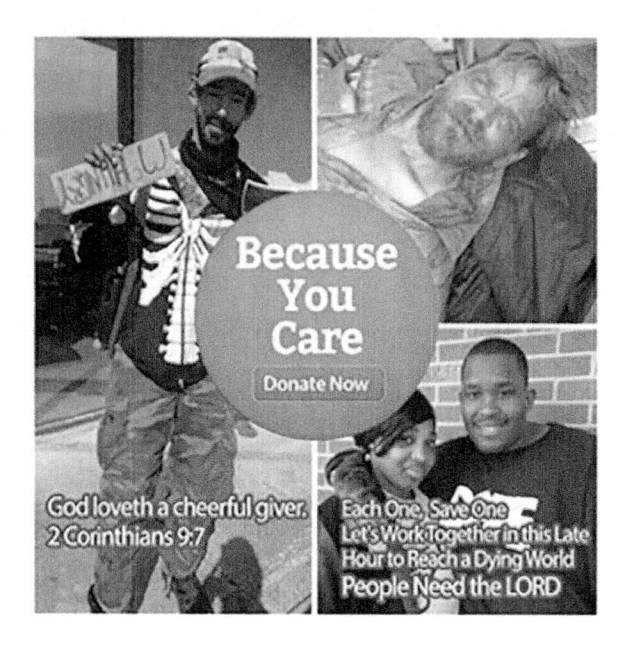

Learn How You Can Participate:

See the "Because You Care" link at SafeGuardYourSoul.com
safeguardyoursoul.com/because-you-care/

Made in the USA
Middletown, DE
07 September 2021